95797

P9-DNP-556

Valued Landscapes
of the Far North

Valued Landscapes
of the Far North

A Geographical Journey through Denali National Park

Eugene J. Palka

ROWMAN & LITTLEFIELD PUBLISHERS, INC.
Lanham • Boulder • New York • Oxford

ROWMAN & LITTLEFIELD PUBLISHERS, INC.

Published in the United States of America
by Rowman & Littlefield Publishers, Inc.
4720 Boston Way, Lanham, Maryland 20706
http://www.rowmanlittlefield.com

12 Hid's Copse Road
Cumnor Hill, Oxford OX2 9JJ, England

British Library Cataloguing in Publication Information Available

ISBN 0-8476-9822-X (cloth)
ISBN 0-8476-9823-8 (paperback)

Printed in the United States of America

♾™ The paper used in this publication meets the minimum requirements of American
National Standard for Information Sciences—Permanence of Paper for Printed Library
Materials, ANSI Z39.48-1992.

Dedicated to
the park rangers, naturalists, administrators, and maintenance
personnel of Denali National Park and Preserve. Thanks to
your uncompromising standards and unwavering sense of
stewardship, you have managed to conserve this special place
for enjoyment by future generations.

Contents

Maps

Figures

Photographs

Acknowledgments

During the course of my research and the publication process for this book, I have been the beneficiary of superb mentoring, scholarly advice, tremendous cooperation, and moral and financial support. I am extremely grateful to all those who helped to make this project a reality.

Professors Wilbert M. Gesler, John W. Florin, Stephen S. Birdsall, Thomas M. Whitmore, and Deb Bialeschki were intimately involved with my graduate studies during the course of my doctoral program at the University of North Carolina at Chapel Hill, and each of them shared my enthusiasm for Denali National Park. Their advice and guidance were invaluable during the initial stages of my research, and various parts of this book reflect their individual insights and wisdom. I am also indebted to several other professors at UNC for contributing to my research and development. My sincere thanks to Melinda S. Meade, Stephen J. Walsh, David R. Butler, James H. Johnson, and Doug Eyre for sharing their expertise and further whetting my appetite for geography. Finally, the generous support of the Eyre Fund enabled me to return to Alaska on two occasions to complete necessary fieldwork.

This publication surely would not have been possible without the cooperation of the National Park Service (NPS) and my friends serving with the NPS in Denali National Park. I am surely thankful for the cheerful manner in which they assisted me during my fieldwork, and for providing me with unlimited access to their historical records, photographs, and special collections. I am especially grateful to Linda Toms, Jane Tranel, Ken Kehrer, Russ Berry, Tom Martin, Thea Nordling, and Cindy Alverez for their assistance and cooperation.

During the publication process, I have truly enjoyed the professional support and guidance of Susan McEachern, vice president and executive editor, Brenda Hadenfeldt, acquisitions editor, and Karen Johnson, assistant editor. It has been a pleasure to work with them and the superb editorial and production staffs of Rowman & Littlefield Publishers.

Portions of two chapters were previously published as an article in *Historical Geography* and as part of a chapter in *Therapeutic Landscapes: The Dynamic between Place and Wellness* by University Press of America. I am indebted to the editor of the former and the publisher of the latter for granting me permission to reprint sections of the previous article and chapter.

Arthur Richard Bloor, a noted wildlife photographer, accompanied me during parts of my fieldwork, and several of his outstanding photographs appear in this book. I am also grateful to my colleague and friend Jon Malinowski for his technical assistance.

Finally, I would be remiss if I did not acknowledge the continual devotion of my wife, Cindy, my son, Gene, and my daughter, Holly. Together we discovered the peace and tranquillity of Denali National Park during our years in Alaska, and they continue to share my passion for Denali long after we moved away. I will always be grateful for our good fortune to have experienced this pristine setting as a family, and I am convinced that we will always cherish the memories of those special times in that special place.

1

Introduction

Geographers have traditionally employed the concept of "place" as an integrating theme and as a means to restrict their focus. They are concerned with places, in both the general and the particular sense. In the case of the former, a desert, a plateau, or a tropical rain forest represents a specific class or genus. Cities, suburbs, or rural areas might also fall into the category. In the latter case, a particular place like Paris, France, or the Mojave Desert, or the Everglades Swamp, or even a particular location within the room of a house might provide the appropriate scale of analysis for geographic inquiry.

Denali National Park is a place that has become increasingly important over the past eighty years for a variety of reasons, including its symbolic value as pristine wilderness and its distinction as part of America's last frontier. This book seeks to uncover the important aspects of this particular place that has been variously categorized as a pristine subarctic ecosystem, national park, wilderness preserve, international biosphere reserve, and therapeutic landscape, to name a few.

My overall goal is to provide an enjoyable and comprehensive geography of this place that is both unique and of increasing importance to Americans and the international community. Within the context of this overall goal, I have two specific objectives: (1) to illuminate those historical, physical, and cultural attributes that contribute to the "spirit of Denali" and (2) to uncover the unique evolution of America's "accessible wilderness" in order to explain how this national park of over eighty years manages to endure nearly one million visitors each summer and, unlike other U.S. national parks, still maintain its pristine wilderness character.

The Setting

Denali National Park and Preserve is located in the heart of interior Alaska (see map 1.1). The park covers more than six million acres and is larger than the state of Massachusetts. The visitor access center, located at the entrance to the park, is more than 125 miles south of Fairbanks and more than 230 miles north of Anchorage. Thus, the park is not only distant from the continental U.S. but is also comfortably separated from Alaska's two largest concentrations of people.

Originally established in 1917 as Mount McKinley National Park, the original purpose of the park was to preserve the region's large mammals for enjoyment by future generations.[1] Consequently, new legislation has been enacted on several occasions to accommodate the wildlife in the region and to maintain the park as an intact ecosystem.

The park's eminence stems from three primary sources: its importance as an international biosphere reserve; its popularity as a distant, wild, and scenic one-of-a-kind national park; and its symbolic value as a vast, pristine wilderness that is a part of America's last frontier. Together, these aspects illuminate Denali's distinctiveness as the largest tract of land in the world that shares simultaneous designations as an international

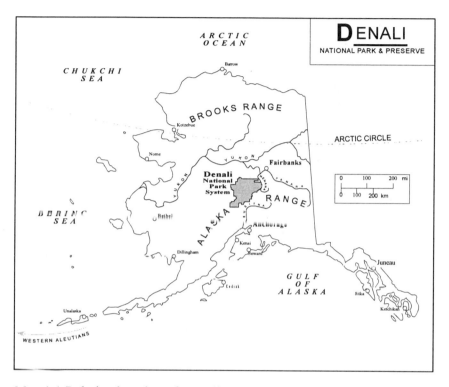

Map 1.1 Relative location of Denali National Park in the interior of Alaska

biosphere reserve, a national park, and a wilderness area.

As an international biosphere reserve, the park provides an ideal area for ecological and environmental research, including baseline studies, because of the tremendous diversity and integrity of biotic communities of plants and animals within this natural ecosystem.[2] Moreover, the park provides unique communities and areas with unusual features of exceptional interest, all within a region that is afforded long-term legal protection from disruption. Denali is currently regarded as the largest intact ecosystem in the world that has been afforded continuous legal protection.[3]

Among the U.S. national parks, Denali National Park is an anomaly. It is visited by nearly one and a half million people each year, yet it remains generally void of any human imprint.

The park boasts a pristine natural setting of varied and undisturbed wildlife, flora, fauna, and landforms. Denali hosts more than 430 species of flowering plants, 157 species of birds, and 37 species of mammals. Predator-prey relationships continue to exist in balance. Perhaps more importantly from a visitor's perspective, wildlife symbolic of wilderness and long driven from its former range in the "lower 48" continues to thrive in Denali National Park. The grizzly bear, wolf, caribou, loon, and golden eagle are most notable among the icons of this wild land and are complemented by moose and Dall sheep.

The term "cosmic landscape" was coined by John Jakle in 1987 to refer to the Grand Canyon and other landscapes that appear to many people as seemingly infinite spaces, lifeless, repetitive, and predictable.[4] By contrast, Denali is varied, unpredictable, colorful, and teeming with life. The alpine glaciers, taiga, high alpine tundra, glacial and clear rivers and streams, and dominant mountains meld to produce breathtaking landscapes that are aethestically pleasing as well as awe-inspiring. The underlying Athapaskan myths about the origin and significance of Denali combine with the spectacular natural setting to provide a landscape that is peaceful, harmonious, and thought-provoking. Fortunately, since Denali's establishment in 1917 (long before Alaska's statehood), legislation has effectively controlled access, limited activities, and even conditioned human behavior to respect the unique place as a "valued environment."[5]

Constructing a Geography

Geography is often regarded as an integrative discipline, as it seeks to describe and explain the variable character of the surface of the earth as the home of humanity. Producing a geography of Denali National Park involves incorporating aspects of both human and physical geographical information from literature sources as well as observations during fieldwork.

Moreover, it also entails integrating knowledge from other disciplines (like history, geology, botany, anthropology, ecology, and zoology) with which geography overlaps, in order to eventually produce a synthesis of what is where and why.

A wide variety of publications, reports, and historical documents contain information concerning Denali's historical, physical, and cultural geography. Much of the information, however, is contained within larger works addressing a region of Alaska or even the entire state. Consequently, the geographical information from such sources must be placed in historical context and requires careful analysis and integration in order to contribute to this construction of a wholistic place geography.

This book is the culmination of research conducted via a comprehensive review of the literature, an archival search, and extensive fieldwork. The materials incorporated include government documents (including materials from the U.S. House, the U.S. Congress, specific Congressional Acts, reports from the U.S. Department of the Interior and the National Park Service, the annual reports of the governor of Alaska and the park superintendent, and early explorations conducted by the U.S. Geological Survey) and contemporary publications of both an academic and a popular nature.

Chronicles of the Journey

Following this introduction, chapter 2, the historical geography of Denali National Park, is designed to capture how the place has evolved. It examines the history of the park and specific phases of development, which correspond to advancements in transportation technology, the latter making the park more accessible and resulting in a gradual but continuous increase in visitors. The historical geography is an integral part of any place, if one accepts that all places are "becoming." That is, the current place has been shaped by past processes, human and natural, and ongoing processes will determine the nature and character of the place in the future.

The historical geography of the park is approached via a review of the literature, an archival search, and by generating specific historical maps. Information sources are distributed among three general locations: the library systems at major universities; special collections at the University of Alaska, Fairbanks; and within the library, museum, and historical files in Denali National Park. The intent is to examine and highlight the unique evolution of the park's natural and cultural landscape, to reconstruct the morphology of the park's boundaries, and to identify the impacts of transportation innovations on the park's accessibility and subsequent visitor pressure.

I primarily employ a "cross-sectional" historical approach.[6] In this regard, I examine and reconstruct the geography of the park for particular "time slices": the pre-park era (12,000BP-1917); the railroad era (1921-1956); the gravel road era (1957-1971); and the highway era (1972-present). Reconstructing the historical geography of the park ultimately seeks to answer two critical questions. Why does Denali bear far less of a human imprint than any other U.S. national park? Perhaps more important, how has the park been able to maintain its pristine wilderness character in light of nearly one million visitors each year?

Maps are employed to highlight two important themes in the development of the park: accessibility and boundary morphology. Initial maps reveal the remote and inaccessible character of the park. Subsequent maps show the park becoming more accessible through developments in transportation technology. Visitor statistics are presented to confirm the drastic increase in visitor pressure coincident with improved access. Maps that focus on the park's boundaries and internal dimensions are designed to capture the areal expansion of the park and specifically address where, when, and why the park was enlarged.

Much of the literature reviewed on the historical geography

of Denali was comprised of secondary sources. The archival search, however, was devoted to uncovering primary sources. In regard to the latter, I focused on original government documents concerning the establishment and initial operation of the park and subsequent legislation that implemented specific management strategies or expanded or redefined park boundaries. I also reviewed the annual reports of the first superintendent of the park and his annual reports to the director of the National Park Service. The annual reports of the governor of Alaska to the Department of the Interior from 1925 through 1959 were also researched. Other primary sources that were assessed and employed include original accounts of the early explorations of the interior of Alaska (and the present-day park region) by the United States Army and later by the United States Geological Survey (USGS). In addition, I interviewed Eleanor Lundee (daughter of the late Charles Sheldon, the founder of Mount McKinley National Park) on several occasions and acquired personal insights about her late father.

Chapter 3 examines the physical geography of the park. The physical geography of a place is more than its setting or backdrop. It is an integral aspect of the place, providing visual and other sensory stimuli that encourage interaction and focus and provide the context for a memorable experience. The aspects of the physical geography that are presented herein are those aspects that are of interest to the average visitor to the park and are largely contained within the activity space of the visitors. The emphasis is on description and to a lesser degree on process, insofar as the former enhances understanding on the part of the visitor, thus contributing to the retention of particular images or sensations associated with the place. My experience with hundreds of shuttle bus riders confirms that aspects of the physical landscape that are not understood are easily forgotten. Understanding, however, enhances retention because it encourages the visitor to impart meaning to the scene. Moreover, it enables the visitor to place a particular image into perspective, at least within the context of one's own experience in other parks or wilderness areas. Thus, a new reference point is established in the mind.

The physical geography of the park is examined by way of a literature review and extensive fieldwork, which included photography and mapping. Although the entire park is addressed in a general sense, the focus is on the unique aspects of the physical environment that the average visitor routinely experiences and that subsequently serve to distinguish Denali from other places. Hence, the core area is the ninety-mile road corridor that is traversed by the park's daily shuttle bus system. The physical geography is descriptive, as well as process oriented, and is concerned with aspects of the park's climate, geomorphology, hydrology, vegetative cover, and mammals. Deviating from more traditional geographic views of the physical landscape as a stage upon which the human drama unfolds, or as a static setting or backdrop, I regard it as an active entity, dynamic in nature and inviting human interaction and response. As such, understanding and appreciating the physical geography of Denali is fundamental to discerning the human-environment interaction and recognizing the character of the place.

The specific aspects of the park's physical geography that I address are those that generated the most interest among the visitors to the park. The interest in specific aspects of the physical landscape or wildlife was substantiated via interviews, questionnaires, and participant observation employed during the conduct of my fieldwork in the park. As such, I sought to map and photograph specific phenomena during my fieldwork. In addition, I sought to photograph key aspects at different times during the summer tourist season. I subsequently employed a literature review to describe the selected phenomena. Moreover, I included a cursory explanation of the processes involved in the making of a current landscape feature. Greater understanding prompts increased retention of the physical geography of the park and ultimately contributes to an enduring sense of place. On numerous occasions I observed visitors sharing information about the origin and/or significance of specific aspects of the physical environment. These conversations help to contribute to consensus images of the place and are mutually reinforcing.

The maps of the physical geography of the park serve to highlight the distinguishing features of Denali. I specifically address the river systems, the mountains, the extent of glaciation, the vegetation regimes, and the ranges of the park's most celebrated mammals.

Chapter 4 presents a cultural geography of Denali from both a traditional and a "new" perspective. The traditional perspective focuses on the enduring cultural landscape theme. The new perspective seeks to uncover how people experience Denali and why they learn to value the place. Additionally, I examine Denali as a therapeutic landscape, functioning and enduring as much because of the human interaction and meaning people impart to it as because of its pristine nature.

From the traditional perspective, my emphasis is on the description and evolution of the cultural landscape. My fieldwork involved photographing and mapping various aspects of material culture, visitor activities, and landscape change. Analyses from the perspective of the so-called new cultural geography are interpretive and explanatory and involved the use of participant observation, surveys, and informal interviews. It is within the context of this new cultural geography that I seek to substantiate Denali's reputation as a therapeutic landscape.

The concluding chapter advocates the use of place geographies to reveal the various layers of meaning places possess, and to provide a greater understanding of how places become and endure. It also reasserts the therapeutic nature of pristine wilderness areas and emphasizes the utility of visitor access and control strategies to better manage irreplaceable natural resources like Denali. Finally, several thought-provoking, if not controversial, concepts are borrowed from the literature of the new cultural geography and used to reexamine the visitor experience within the park.

Notes

1. Charles Sheldon, *The Wilderness of Denali* (New York: Scribner's, 1930). The idea of a game preserve was always foremost in Sheldon's mind. The common misconception is that the initial impetus for the park was to preserve Mount McKinley.

2. Michael Batisse, "The Biosphere Reserve: A Tool for Environmental Conservation and Management," *Environmental Conservation* 9, no. 2 (1982): 101-111.

3. United States Department of the Interior, National Park Service, General Management Plan, Land Protection Plan, Wilderness Suitability Review (Denali Park, Alaska: National Park Service, 1987).

4. John A. Jakle, *The Visual Elements of Landscape* (Amherst: University of Massachusetts Press, 1987).

5. John R. Gold and Jacquelin A. Burgess, *Valued Environments* (London: Allen & Unwin, 1982). The term is also routinely applied to historic landmarks, areas of scenic beauty and unique vegetative regimes, and wildlife habitats.

6. H. C. Darby, ed., *An Historical Geography of England before AD 1800* (Cambridge: Cambridge University Press, 1936). Darby originally developed the "cross-sectional" approach in 1936 and subsequently incorporated the approach in dozens of works, spanning a career of over fifty years.

2

Historical Geography

Among U.S. national parks, Alaska's Denali National Park and Wilderness Preserve is an anomaly. First, the park encompasses an "internationally significant subarctic ecosystem that serves as the baseline for study of comparable environments around the world."[1] Second, it is the largest public land in America that is simultaneously designated as a national park, a wilderness area, and an international biosphere reserve. Third, the park bears far less of a human imprint than any national park in the continental United States, with over 97 percent of its total acreage suitable as wilderness. Fourth, despite the vast wilderness, the park is accessible to people of all ages thanks to a unique visitor access and shuttle bus plan not found in other national parks.

Denali includes more than six million acres and is located in the interior of Alaska. Its natural landscape is varied, colorful, and awe-inspiring. Often called "an island in time," Denali National Park is also the largest example of an entire ecosystem that has been afforded continuous legal protection, thus ensuring the preservation of its wilderness character.[2] Additionally, the multicolored tundra, featuring countless varieties of mosses, lichens, wildflowers, and berries; the looming mountains of the Alaska Range, laced with glaciers and braided rivers and streams; and glacial erratics resting upon tundra more than thirty miles from their original sources make Denali a sightseer's paradise. And yet, while nearly one million people visit each year, the human imprint is negligible.

When asked to compare Denali to other national parks, the vast majority of visitors (most of whom had visited numerous other national parks) interviewed or surveyed by the author describe Denali as a "one-of-a-kind national park."[3] This perception prompts the following question: How can any national park of more than eighty years endure an onslaught of visitors each summer and maintain its wilderness character? The answer to this question has implications for management strategies in other national parks, and can best be answered by reviewing the historical geography of Denali National Park.

Early Exploration

Based on artifactual remains determined to be older than 10,500BP, most archaeologists concur that humans set foot in the area that is now Denali Park about 12,000 years ago, near the end of the most recent Ice Age.[4] Nevertheless, evidence of a Native American presence at Denali is almost nonexistent. The existing archaeological remains suggest that the Athapaskan Indians relied on the Denali area only as a large mammal hunting ground, particularly for caribou and moose.[5] Permanent village sites were located in lower, warmer, and more sheltered locations, and invariably along fish-producing rivers.[6] The Athapaskans practiced a subsistence lifestyle, relying chiefly upon fish and big game for survival. Since most of the rivers and streams throughout Denali are glacial, they are not nearly as productive fisheries as streams and rivers outside the park. Moreover, navigable rivers are the keys to mobility in the subarctic environment. Whether one is traveling by canoe or raft in the summer or by dogsled during the winter, rivers provide the major thoroughfares. Consequently, native people settled along the major navigable rivers throughout Alaska. We can conclude then that Native Americans used Denali's six million acres mainly for seasonal hunting and had little if any enduring impact on the natural landscape.

Alaska's interior remained unexplored by outsiders until 1794. Captain George Vancouver, an English navigator, is generally credited with being the first white man to give an account of the Alaskan interior.[7] Vancouver surveyed the Cook Inlet, about 130 miles south of present-day Denali National Park, mentioning the "distant stupendous mountains covered with snow and detached from one another."[8] Most likely, his observation focused on Mounts McKinley and Foraker. The Denali area, however, remained unexplored for the next century because of the remote location, rugged terrain, and harsh climate.

As often happens in frontier regions, mineral deposits served as the first major attraction to the Denali region. Fur traders Alfred Mayo and Arthur Harper journeyed along the Tanana River in 1878 and returned with news of gold and "a great ice mountain."[9] Their report encouraged exploration of the Denali region, first by Frank Densmore and his gold-prospecting party in 1889.[10] Densmore enthusiastically wrote about the great ice mountain, which became known as "Densmore's Mountain."[11] In 1896, William A. Dickey, one of two thousand or so gold seekers who arrived at Cook Inlet, reported his adventures in the *New York Sun* (January 24, 1897). He renamed Densmore's Mountain as "Mount McKinley" to honor presidential candidate William McKinley, who—like Dickey—favored the gold standard.[12] Prospectors did not find what they were seeking, however, until 1905 when gold was discovered in the Kantishna Hills to the northwest of Mount McKinley. Activity flourished for about a year until miners realized the limited extent of gold deposits and abandoned the area for more promising fields.

Beginning in 1898, the USGS officially surveyed and explored the region.[13] Several years later Charles Sheldon, an accomplished naturalist, hunter, and conservationist in the Teddy Roosevelt mold, began to promote the idea of designating the region as a nature preserve. Lured by reports of big game animals (especially Dall sheep), in 1906 Sheldon became the first Caucasian to explore the Denali Region extensively, conducting a six-week trek and returning for a longer expedition between August 1, 1907, and June 11, 1908. During this second trip, Sheldon and his guide, Harry Karstens, built a small cabin along the Toklat River where they spent the winter. Sheldon wanted to establish a park to protect the region's large mammals.[14] Consequently, he spent most of 1907 hunting and studying appropriate boundaries for the game refuge.[15] Upon returning to the lower 48 in 1908, Sheldon convinced the Boone and Crockett Club's Game Committee, of which he was the chair, to launch a vigorous campaign to establish a nature preserve near Mount McKinley.[16]

Sheldon wanted the park to be called Denali, a local Indian word for the mountain meaning "the high one" or "the great one."[17] Alaska judge James Wickersham and Nevada senator Key Pitman, however, introduced congressional bills in April 1916 bearing the name "Mount McKinley National Park."[18] On February 26, 1917, largely through the efforts of Sheldon, President Woodrow Wilson signed into law the bill establishing Mount McKinley National Park.[19]

Morphology of a Remote National Park

At first, Mount McKinley National Park had no visitor facilities, not even a rudimentary access road into the park. Congress did not provide funds to staff the park until 1921.[20] Original park superintendent Harry Karstens and his staff of one ranger operated out of Nenana, about sixty miles north of the park.[21] By the end of that year, however, the Alaska Railroad, subsidized by the federal government, extended its main line south from Nenana to Mount McKinley Park, where a depot was established. The link with Nenana enabled Karstens to relocate his headquarters inside the park to a site near Riley Creek in 1922. The superintendent's dwelling and office were constructed in close proximity to the railroad depot, using logs and lumber recovered from deserted construction camps along the railroad (see photograph 2.1).[22]

The next year, Karstens, Ranger Powless, and two prospectors pioneered efforts to develop a crude twelve-mile road from the park entrance to a new camp on the Savage River.[23] Thirty-four out of forty total park visitors stayed at this camp (see photograph 2.2) during the summer of 1923.[24]

In the same year, the main railroad line between Seward, Anchorage, and Fairbanks was completed, prompting improvements to the McKinley Park depot, the most celebrated stop along the main line (see photograph 2.3). Additionally, Congress appropriated $5,000 for road construction from the park entrance to Wonder Lake.[25] Before this, annual park visitors to the park numbered fewer than fifty. In less than five years after the completion of these new transportation links, visitors increased to five hundred per year.[26]

The park's cultural landscape developed slowly over the next fifty years, leaving few enduring imprints on the natural landscape. Most improvements were concentrated in a small built-up area extending from the visitor access center at the park entrance to the park headquarters. This area comprises less than 0.1 percent of the total park area (see map 2.1). Here, the National Park Service added permanent campsites, walking paths, and nature trails.

Photograph 2.1 Park headquarters building as it appeared in 1939 (National Park Service)

Park and railroad development went hand in hand from 1921 to 1957. The railroad provided the only access to the remote park. The Alaska Railroad Company transported supplies and materials for the construction of the earliest park buildings and facilities. What is more important, the railroad financed, built, and ran a hotel at the park, using it as one of three overnight stops along the 470-mile route between Fairbanks and Seward.[27] Thus a reciprocal relationship developed between the railroad and the park: the railroad provided access and accommodations while the park became a major attraction for passengers. By 1956, yearly visits climbed to 5,122.[28]

In 1957, the park began a transition from being exclusively a "railroad park," to one that was accessible, albeit to a limited degree, by automobile. With the completion of the Denali

Photograph 2.2 The Savage River camp as it appeared in 1927 (National Park Service)

Highway (Route 8), which linked the park to the Richardson Highway via a 135-mile stretch between Cantwell and Paxon (see map 2.2), the park received more than twice as many visitors as the previous year, increasing to 10,612.[29] Motorists could now travel the "roundabout" route to the park, some 330 miles from Fairbanks or some 425 miles from Anchorage.[30] Although nothing but a gravel road, the Denali Highway effectively enabled motorists to reach the park for the first time. Previously, automobiles could only be uploaded onto flatcars and transported to the park by rail (see photograph 2.4). Route 8 was rough and time-consuming to travel, and it offered few services, but many visitors accepted the inconveniences willingly. Between 1957 and 1971, annual visits increased from 10,662 to 58,342.[31]

Without question, the greatest stimulus to park visitation was the completion of the paved Anchorage-Fairbanks Highway in 1971 (see map 2.3). Renamed the George Parks Highway in 1975 after a former territorial governor, the 323-mile road provided the first "direct" automobile link to the park.[32] Construction of the Parks Highway began in 1959. It was completed in 1971, paralleling the older Alaska railroad route between Anchorage and Fairbanks.[33] Almost immediately, it rendered the Denali Highway obsolete. Anchorage residents were now only 237 miles from the park entrance, while Fairbanksans were only 121 miles away. By traveling the new road, motorists from Fairbanks saved 209 miles, while those traveling from Anchorage saved 237 miles. Whereas visitors to the park numbered 58,342 in 1971, the number of annual visitors increased to 306,017 in 1972, to 514,579 by 1980, and

Photograph 2.3 The McKinley Park depot in 1939 (National Park Service)

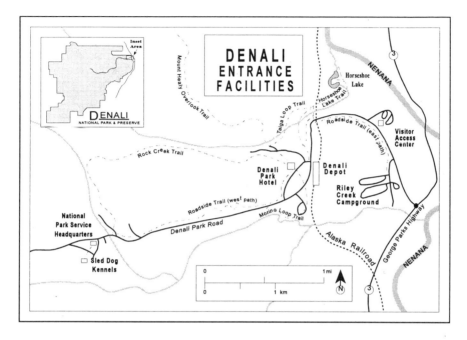

Map 2.1 The built-up area of Denali National Park

surpassed 1,000,000 by 1986.[34] Thus the paved highway made the park more accessible. This increased accessibility prompted immediate regulations and legislation to protect the wildlife, vegetation, and scenic beauty of the park, while adapting to more visitors. Denali's planners and administrators had long anticipated the impact of the highway on park visitations, and to their credit, numerous proposals were carefully staffed prior to the completion of the Parks Highway.

The Impact of Legislation

Anticipating the tremendous increase in park use that highway completion would bring, the National Park Service began to explore alternatives to ensure that additional visitors would not

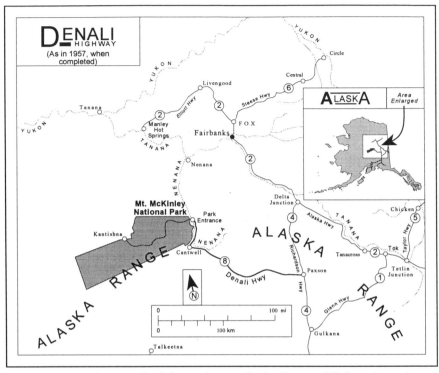

Map 2.2 The Denali Highway (Route 8), the first road link to the park

alter the park nor even place added stress on the natural environment. After reviewing other national parks where improved access prompted a dramatic increase in visitor pressure and subsequent environmental degradation, the Park Service in Denali conducted several internal studies and eventually decided to implement a controlled access system restricting private vehicle traffic to the fourteen-mile stretch of road between the park entrance and the Savage River bridge. Free shuttle bus service was established beyond that point. Every half-hour visitors could board the bus and make round trips to the Eielson Visitor Center or Wonder Lake (see Map 2.4). The bus also enabled visitors to get on or off virtually anywhere along the route, which remained a narrow dirt road. The shuttle bus system proved effective in that it provided access yet precluded disturbance to the flora

Photograph 2.4 A privately owned automobile arriving at the park by flatcar in 1950 (National Park Service)

and fauna. It also maintained the pristine wilderness setting beyond the Savage River, essentially preserving the integrity of this wild land. Unique to Denali, the shuttle bus system has proved to be an innovative solution to the historical challenge of trying to attain a balance between providing public access to wilderness areas and preserving the resource for enjoyment by future generations.

Bearing in mind that the original purpose of Mount McKinley National Park was to preserve the region's large mammals, it was necessary to enact new legislation on several occasions to accommodate wildlife and maintain the park as an intact ecosystem. To incorporate prime caribou and Dall sheep range and breeding grounds, Congress agreed to extend the park boundaries in 1922, east from the Sanctuary to the Nenana River, and again in 1932, west to Wonder Lake.[35] To host other activities that were not compatible with the wilderness character of the park, the state of Alaska created the 324,240-acre Denali State Park next to the southeastern federal park boundary in 1970.[36]

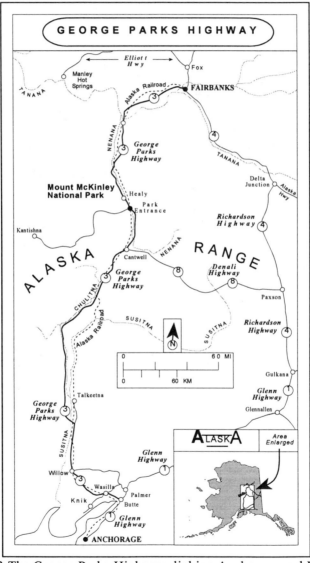

Map 2.3 The George Parks Highway, linking Anchorage and Fairbanks

In the late 1970s, proposals called for further expansion of Mount McKinley National Park to include scenic areas and critical wildlife habitat that had been left outside the original boundaries.[37] The most extensive piece of such legislation came on December 2, 1980, when President Jimmy Carter signed the Alaska National Interest Lands Conservation Act (ANILCA) into law. Briefly summarized, ANILCA expanded the park to the north, west, and south by a total of 2,426,000 acres. It also included an additional 330,000 acres in two separate pieces within the Denali National Preserve. There, a wider range of uses was permitted. The act also retained Mount McKinley as the official name for the continent's highest peak and renamed the entire park Denali National Park and Preserve (see photographs 2.5 and 2.6), recognizing the longstanding Native American local toponymy.[38] The government's noble gesture actually makes little sense to Athapaskans, who use the term Denali, meaning "the high one" or "the great one," to refer to the great mountain, not the six million acres surrounding it. Nevertheless, despite this specific, inherent contradiction, conservationists and biologists who had long felt that straight, political boundaries were inconsistent with protecting a complete ecosystem hailed ANILCA as a success.[39]

Map 2.5 depicts the three primary divisions of the current park. The "national park wilderness" is the most strictly controlled area and is the original Mount McKinley National Park. Established in 1917 as a wildlife refuge, it continues to be managed to maintain the undeveloped wilderness parkland character.[40] The areas designated as national park to the north, west, and south of the "wilderness" area were added by ANILCA in 1980 and allow customary and traditional subsistence use by local residents.[41] The "national preserve," located in the northwest and southwest sections, also allows sport hunting, trapping, and fishing, in addition to subsistence uses.[42]

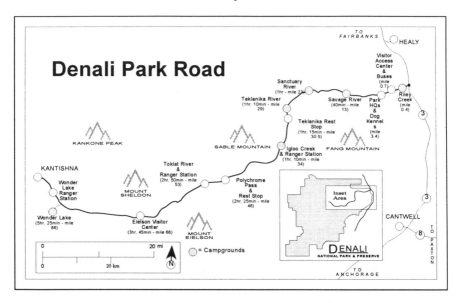

Map 2.4 The Denali Park Road extending from the entrance to Wonder Lake and Kantishna

The most significant piece of international legislation influencing Denali was passed by the United Nations Educational, Scientific, and Cultural Organization (UNESCO) in 1976, designating the park as an "international biosphere reserve" that could contribute to the preservation of biodiversity worldwide.[43] UNESCO recognized that conservation is not merely accomplished by protecting a single species, but by preserving the full array of habitats where species live.[44] Intact ecosystems like Denali Park are invaluable because they provide a standard against which human impacts on the environment can be measured, essentially serving as "global benchmarks of ecological health."[45] Unlike many of the biosphere reserves that were afforded no legal protection prior to designation, Denali has long been protected by more stringent federal legislation. As such, UNESCO was able to superimpose a biosphere reserve, acre for acre on Denali National Park, confirming that the human imprint on the park has been negligible.

Photograph 2.5 One of the earliest signs bearing the original name as Mount McKinley National Park (National Park Service)

Denali National Park Today

Denali Park attracted more than 1.3 million visitors in 1992.[46] This steady increase in annual visitors can be attributed to further advances in transportation technology and Alaska's booming tourist industry. Visitors arrive by auto or train from either Fairbanks or Anchorage (see photograph 2.7). Most are out-of-state residents who fly to Fairbanks or Anchorage international airports. Others come via the Alaska Marine Highway or the Princess Cruise Line ships that travel through the Inside Passage from Seattle or Canadian ports. Princess and other large travel companies offer multiple tour packages that routinely feature a visit to Denali. These particular visitors stay in

Photograph 2.6 The current entrance sign reflecting the name change of the park

the park for a very short time.

Principal attractions of the park include its wildlife, scenic landforms, Mount McKinley, and the wilderness experience. Since the establishment of the park, Denali's wildlife remains the featured attraction. Of the thirty-seven species of mammals, the most popular have always been bears, caribou, Dall sheep, moose, and wolves. As clarified in the *Denali Alpenglow*, however, "Denali is not a safari park or zoo where wildlife are restricted to places where they can easily be seen. On the contrary, Denali is a natural habitat where animals can roam as they choose, anywhere within the park's six million acres and beyond."[47] Consequently, visitors often speculate about their chances of viewing the wildlife. It is significant

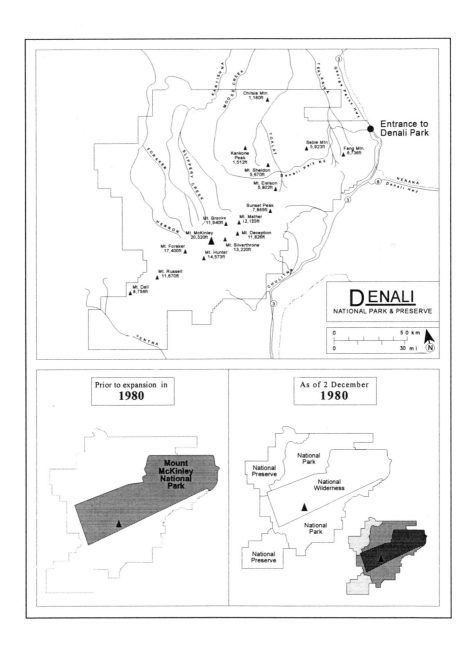

Map 2.5 Primary subdivisions of Denali National Park and Preserve

to note that the park's shuttle bus system, with about forty pairs of eyes per bus, is an extremely effective means of assuring visitors that they will be successful in their quest to view the park's wildlife.[48] Perhaps more importantly, wildlife disturbance has been minimized. The presence of wolves and grizzly bears, undisputed symbols of the wild yet long vanished from other national parks, serves as testimony.

In terms of being a featured attraction of the park, Mount McKinley is a close second to the wildlife. At 20,320 feet, Mount McKinley is the highest mountain in North America and has the highest vertical rise of any mountain in the world. Aside from attracting visitors because of its scenic beauty and grandeur, Mount McKinley lures renowned climbers from all over the world. In 1992 alone, a total of 1,068 people from

Photograph 2.7 Visitors arriving by train at the park's railroad depot

twenty-three countries attempted to reach the summit.[49] The "high one" has long posed the ultimate challenge to climbers around the world because of its harsh environment and unpredictable weather.[50] Nevertheless, if past statistics are any indication, it appears that expert mountain climbers from around the world will continue to accept the Mount McKinley challenge in future years.

In *The Nature of Denali*, Sheri Forbes calls Denali National Park the "crown jewel" of the U.S. National Park system and one of the "few remaining intact ecosystems on earth."[51] While I strongly agree on both accounts, it is not possible to prove her first claim objectively. Nevertheless, it can be said that Denali is a one-of-a-kind national park. It is unique in terms of its intact flora, fauna, and landform ecosystem. More importantly, it has felt less of a human impact than any national park in the continental United States. This is despite the fact that it has endured more than eighteen million visitors since its establishment in 1917 (and more than a million visitors a year since 1986). A review of Denali's historical geography provides several explanations.

First, during the pre-national park era, native Athapaskans sought permanent settlement in regions less environmentally harsh than the Denali region. Thus, for more than twelve thousand years the region was subject only to seasonal hunting of big game animals. Second, Denali's remoteness and inaccessibility helped to preserve biodiversity. In spite of multiple advances in transportation technology, Denali remains distant from the continental United States and comfortably separated from Alaska's concentrations of potential visitors. Third, the Alaskan climate limits the majority of park visitation to three months (June through August). Undoubtedly, the nine-month "recovery period" helps the park maintain an undisturbed natural state. Fourth, legislation and regulations governing activities within Denali were firmly in place prior to significant visitor pressure. Unlike national parks in the lower 48, visitor increase was gradual, in response to the slow, incremental nature of transportation developments.[52] As such, the impact of increased access could be easily anticipated, and through prescribed legislation, an increased number of visitors could be accommodated. Consequently, visitor behavior was conditioned almost from the outset, and the natural system never experienced any irreversible setbacks as we have seen in other national parks.[53] Moreover, management strategies employed in Denali could benefit from the lessons learned in other national parks where visitor crises occurred many years earlier. As Cecil D. Andrus, secretary of the U.S. Department of the Interior, noted: "The premise of the Alaska lands legislation held out to the American people has always been that whole ecosystems would be preserved, and that the land management errors of the Lower 48 States would not be repeated again."[54]

Thus, Denali's hostile environment and remote location have been fortuitous. In addition, appropriate laws and regulations prevented irreversible, human-induced impacts and proved successful in preserving Denali more completely than any national park in the continental United States. The current challenge, however, is to keep it this way. There simply are no other places within the United States with such large, diverse, and intact ecosystems that are simultaneously free from human disruption and alteration yet accessible for public enjoyment. Denali may represent a last chance. Ongoing significant efforts should be made to preserve this "island in time" for all time.

Notes

1. National Park Service, *General Management Plan, Land Protection Plan, Wilderness Suitability Review* (Denali Park, Alaska: National Park Service, 1987), 74.

2. National Park Service, *General Management Plan*. See also Rick McIntyre, *Denali National Park: An Island in Time* (Santa Barbara, Calif.: Sequoia Communications, 1986). The expression alludes to Denali's ability to endure millions of visitors over the past seventy years, without any visible change in the park's natural landscape. Unlike in other national parks, the human imprint in Denali is negligible.

3. Based on the author's fieldwork and sample of over two hundred tourists during the 1993 summer season.

4. National Park Service, *General Management Plan, Land Protection Plan, Wilderness Suitability Review*, 136. See also Janie Freeburg and Deana Ackland, eds., *Insight Guide: Alaska* (Singapore: APA Publications, 1991), 205.

5. William E. Brown, *Denali: Symbol of the Alaskan Wild* (Virginia Beach: Donning Company Publishers, 1933), 17. See also Sheri Forbes, *The Nature of Denali* (Denali National Park: Alaska Natural History Association, 1992), 6.

6. Alfred H. Brooks, *The Mount McKinley Region, Alaska*, USGS Professional Paper 70 (Washington, D.C.: Government Printing Office), 216. See also Freeburg and Ackland, *Insight Guide: Alaska*, 205. This same settlement pattern is common among other Indian tribes throughout interior Alaska.

7. Brooks, *The Mount McKinley Region*, 23. See also National Park Service, *General Management Plan, Land Protection Plan, Wilderness Suitability Review*, 137.

8. Elaine Rhode, "Denali Country," *Alaska Geographic* 15, no. 3 (1988): 13.

9. Rhode, "Denali Country," 13. See also Brooks, *The Mount McKinley Region*, 25.

10. Steve Buskirk, *Denali: The Story behind the Scenery* (Las Vegas: KC Publications, 1989), 40. The time lag between Mayo's report and Densmore's subsequent exploration is attributed to the inaccessibility of the McKinley region and the availability of more accessible and well-established prospecting alternatives elsewhere during the period.

11. Buskirk, *Denali*, 40.

12. Buskirk, *Denali*, 42. Also see Brooks, *The Mount McKinley Region*, 26. Ironically, the late President McKinley never even set foot in Alaska, much less saw the mountain that was named after him.

13. The original USGS reports are included in U.S. House, 56th Congress, 1st Session, 1900, Document No. 5, Twentieth Annual Report of the USGS, 1899, part VII: "Explorations in Alaska in 1898." Specifically covering the Denali Region are: G. H. Eldridge, "A reconnaissance in the Sushitna Basin and adjacent territory, Alaska, in 1898," 1-29; J. E. Spurr, "A reconnaissance in southwestern Alaska in 1898," 31-264; W. C. Mendenhall, " A reconnaissance from Resurrection Bay to the Tanana, Alaska, in 1898," 265-340; and A. H. Brooks, "A reconnaissance in the White and Tanana Basins, Alaska, in 1898," 425-494.

14. Eleanor Lunde, daughter of Charles Sheldon, personal interview, March 4, 1994. A common misconception is that the initial motivation for a national park was to preserve the majestic Mount McKinley.

15. Sheldon's own personal account of his year-long research in the

Denali region is provided in *The Wilderness of Denali* (New York: Scribner's, 1930). The book is the published version of Sheldon's field notes and journal entries. The original notes are compiled in the Sheldon Papers, University of Alaska, Fairbanks, Archives. Also see Brown, *Denali*, 79-94, for an excellent synopsis of Sheldon's explorations in the Denali region.

16. Lunde, personal interview, March 4, 1994. Interestingly, a large portion of the Mount McKinley massif was left outside the original park boundaries. See Presidential Proclamation, "Denali National Monument," Proclamation 4616, December 1, 1978.

17. Sheldon, *The Wilderness of Denali*, 389. Also, Lunde, personal interview, March 4, 1994.

18. U.S. House, 64th Congress, 1st Session, May 4, 1916, "Hearing on a Bill to Establish Mount McKinley National Park" (Washington, D.C.: Government Printing Office, 1916); Rhode, "Denali Country," 16.

19. "An Act to Establish the Mount McKinley National Park, in the Territory of Alaska," approved February 26, 1917 (39 stat. 938); Buskirk, *Denali*, 45. A detailed account of Sheldon's efforts and the extensive lobbying that preceded legislation establishing the national park is provided by Brown, *Denali: Symbol of the Alaskan Wild*, 89-94.

20. U.S. Department of the Interior, *Report of the Director of the National Park Service to the Secretary of the Interior for the Fiscal Year Ended June 30, 1921, and the Travel Season 1921* (Washington, D.C.: Government Printing Office), 96; Buskirk, *Denali*, 45.

21. Henry P. Karstens, "Report of the Superintendent of Mount McKinley National Park," in *Report of the Director of the National Park Service to the Secretary of the Interior for Fiscal Year Ended June 30, 1921 and the Travel Season 1921*, 250. The most comprehensive history covering the early years of the park is provided by Brown, *Denali*, 129-153.

22. Karstens, "*Report of the Superintendent*," 146.

23. Karstens, "Report of the Superintendent," 146.

24. U.S. Department of the Interior, *Report of the Director of the National Park Service to the Secretary of the Interior for the Fiscal Year Ended June 30, 1923 and the Travel Season, 1923* (Washington, D.C.: Government Printing Office, 1923), 99; Kim Heacox, In *Denali* (Santa Barbara, Calif.: Jane Freeburg, 1992), 88.

25. Kim Heacox, *The Denali Road Guide* (Denali National Park: Alaska Natural History Association, 1986), 13.

26. Heacox, *The Denali Road Guide*, 89.

27. Alaska Geographic Society, "Riding the Rails to Denali Country," *Alaska Geographic* 15, no. 3 (1988): 63. Also see U.S. Department of the Interior, *The Alaska Railroad Travelogue: Mt. McKinley Park Route* (Washington, D.C.: Government Printing Office, 1928) for an example of how the railroad marketed the park, as well as its rail service.

28. National Park Service, Denali National Park, Alaska, unpublished statistics of visitors to Denali National Park and Preserve, 1940-1992.

29. Denali National Park, unpublished statistics, 1940-1992. The Governor of Alaska, *Annual Report to the Secretary of the Interior for the Fiscal Year Ended June 30, 1958* (Washington, D.C.: Government Printing Office, 1956), 96.

30. Alaska Geographic Society, "Denali Highway," *Alaska Geographic* 10, no. 1 (1983): 123.

31. National Park Service, Denali National Park, Alaska, unpublished statistics.

32. Alaska Geographic Society, "George Parks Highway," *Alaska Geographic* 10, no. 1 (1983): 145.

33. Alaska Geographic Society, "George Parks Highway," 146.

34. Alaska Geographic Society, "George Parks Highway," 156. Also referenced, National Park Service, Denali National Park, Alaska, unpublished statistics, 1940-1992.

35. "An Act To add certain lands to Mount McKinley National Park, Alaska," approved January 30, 1922 (42 Stat. 359); "An Act To revise the boundary of the Mount McKinley National Park, in the Territory of Alaska, and for other purposes," approved March 19, 1932 (47 Stat. 68). Also see Jenny Flynn, "Denali at 75: From Sheep to Shuttle Buses," *Denali Alpenglow* 14 (Summer 1992): 1. The *Denali Alpenglow* is the park's newspaper that is published each year and includes a multitude of current and insightful articles written by the park rangers and administrators.

36. Rhode, "Denali Country," 16.

37. Presidential Proclamation, "Denali National Monument," Proclamation 4616, December 1, 1978. Also McIntyre, *Denali National Park: Island in Time*, 21.

38. U.S. House, 96th Congress, 1st Session, February 1, 6, 7, 8, and 13, 1979, "Alaska National Interest Lands Conservation Act of 1979," Hearings before the Committee on Interior and Insular Affairs, House of Representatives, on H.R. 39 (Washington, D.C.: Government Printing Office, 1979), 63; Buskirk, *Denali*, 46.

39. Flynn, "Denali at 75," 10. ANILCA provided additional lands which essentially serve as a buffer around the park's wilderness area, better protecting the core from the impacts of incompatible uses or resource exploitation in adjacent lands, and ensuring the range of Denali's wildlife is comfortably within the park's protective boundaries.

40. National Park Service, *General Management Plan, Land Protection Plan, Wilderness Suitability Review*, 158-159. Also see USDI, National Park Service, *Denali National Park and Preserve*, brochure and map.

41. National Park Service, *General Management Plan*, 156-157. The law is intended to protect Athapaskans and Alaskan homesteaders who

continue to practice a subsistence lifestyle.

42. National Park Service, *General Management Plan*, 156-157. Because of the inaccessibility, however, limited activities occur in these areas. See also, USDI, National Park Service, *Denali National Park and Preserve*.

43. William P. Gregg, Jr., Stanley L. Krugman, and James D. Wood, Jr., *Proceedings of the Symposium on Biosphere Reserves, September 11-18, 1987, Estes Park, CO*, USA (Atlanta: USDI, National Park Service, 1987), 288. Also Forbes, *The Nature of Denali*, 28. See also Michael Batisse, "The Biosphere Reserve: A Tool for Environmental Conservation and Management," *Environmental Conservation* 9, no. 2 (1982): 101-111.

44. Forbes, *The Nature of Denali*, 28. A more detailed explanation is provided by Michael Batisse, "Action Plan for Biosphere Reserves," *Environmental Conservation* 12, no. 1 (1985): 17-27.

45. Forbes, *The Nature of Denali*, 28. Also Gregg, Krugman, and Wood, *Proceedings of the Symposium on Biosphere Reserves*, 37.

46. National Park Service, Denali National Park, Alaska, unpublished statistics, 1993. Note that since this time the park has changed its methodology for counting visitors.

47. Charlie Loeb, "Wildlife from the Bus Window," *Denali Alpenglow* 14 (Summer 1992): 7. For a comprehensive analysis of Denali's mammals, their habitat, and their range, see Adolph Murie, *Mammals of Denali* (Anchorage: Alaska Natural History Association, 1983), reprinted from *Mammals of Mount McKinley National Park*, Alaska, 1962.

48. Loeb, "Wildlife from the Bus Window," 7. In a one-week study in July 1988, 95 percent of the shuttle bus passengers saw bears; 95 percent saw caribou; 95 percent saw Dall sheep; 82 percent saw moose; and 24 percent saw wolves.

49. Judi Schmitt, "SAR LOG," *Response* 11, no. 4 (1992): 30.

50. Schmitt, "SAR LOG," 30. In 1992 alone, eleven climbers were killed and sixteen were injured while attempting to reach the summit of Mount McKinley.

51. Forbes, *The Nature of Denali*, 29.

52. For example, in 1917 when Mount McKinley Park was established, the following visitor counts were reported: Hot Springs, 135,000; Yellowstone, 35,400; Yosemite, 34,510; Rocky Mountain, 117,186. In 1923, Mount McKinley reported only 34 visitors, compared to the following: Hot Springs, 112,000; Yellowstone, 138,352; Yosemite, 130,046; Rocky Mountain, 218,000. Mount McKinley did not exceed the 100,000-visitor threshold until 1972, by which time these other parks had long surpassed the one million mark. See U.S. Department of the Interior, *Report of the Director of the National Park Service to the Secretary of the Interior for the Fiscal Year Ended June 30, 1923 and the Travel Season, 1923* (Washington, D.C.: Government Printing Office, 1923), 99.

53. See, for example, Lary M. Dilsaver, "Stemming the Flow: The Evolution of Controls on Visitor Numbers and Impact in National Parks," in *The American Environment: Interpretations of Past Geographies*, ed. Lary M. Dilsaver & Craig E. Colten (Lanham, Md: Rowman & Littlefield, 1992), 235-255. This is an excellent interdisciplinary resource that addresses a number of critical environmental issues stemming from unchecked visitor pressure.

54. U.S. House, 96th Congress, 1st Session, February 1, 6, 7, 8, and 13, 1979, "Alaska National Interest Lands Conservation Act of 1979," Hearings before the Committee on Interior and Insular Affairs, House of Representatives, on H.R. 39 (Washington, D.C.: Government Printing Office, 1979), 507.

3

Physical Geography

Visitors perceive Denali National Park and Wilderness Preserve as an anomaly among the U.S. national parks for several reasons. The park is distant from the continental United States, located in the heart of Alaska; it is vast, covering more than six million acres; its northerly location ensures unique landforms, flora, and fauna; and despite more than a million visitors each year, it remains void of any significant human imprint. Denali's near-virgin status has been maintained thanks to two factors. First, as part of the country's last frontier, it is remote from the continental U.S., and distant even from Alaska's population centers, approximately 245 miles north of Anchorage and 121 miles south of Fairbanks. Moreover, it has been relatively inaccessible for most of its history. Second, since its establishment in 1917 as Mount McKinley National Park, legislation has effectively controlled access, limited activities, and even conditioned human behavior to respect the unique place as a valued environment.

The pristine natural setting in Denali is comprised of varied and undisturbed flora, fauna and landforms. Among the testimonies to the wildness of the region are the predator-prey relationships that continue to exist in balance. In addition, the combination of alpine glaciers, taiga, high alpine tundra, glacial and clear rivers and streams, and dominant mountains meld to produce breathtaking landscapes from any visitor's perspective. Often referred to as an island in time, Denali National Park is currently the largest example of an undisturbed ecosystem that has been afforded legal protection from disruption.[1]

Understanding the unique physical geography of Denali enables visitors to comprehend and appreciate the park's selection as an international biosphere reserve and to differentiate its unique physical features and processes from those seen in other national parks. Recognizing what visitors perceive as the distinguishing features of Denali's physical setting takes us one step closer to understanding the place.

Topography

In general terms, topography refers to the surface features and relief of a place. Most discussions of the dominant landforms of the park probably begin with Mount McKinley, which at 20,320 feet is the highest mountain in North America. Considering that the northern base of the mountain rests on the 2,000-foot elevation mark, the mountain rises vertically for over 18,000 feet (see photograph 3.1). This dramatic vertical rise surpasses all other mountains in the world, including Mount Everest.[2] Mount McKinley actually consists of two peaks (known collectively as the Churchill Peaks): a north summit that reaches a height of 19,470 feet and a south summit that attains a height of 20,320 feet.[3] McKinley's granite and slate

Photograph 3.1 Scenic view of the north face of Mount McKinley

core is overlain by ice that is several hundred feet thick, and permanent snowfields cover more than half the mountain.[4]

Located in the southern area of the park, Mount McKinley is the dominant mountain of the Alaska Range. Based on his extensive fieldwork and multiple surveys, geologist Clyde Wahrhaftig described the Alaska Range as a great arcuate mountain wall, about 600 miles long and 60 miles wide (in the vicinity of Mount McKinley), rugged and intensely glaciated throughout its length, and an impenetrable barrier between Alaska's southern coast and its interior.[5] The range dominates the southern portion of Denali National Park, averaging a height of about 9,000 feet, but boasting multiple peaks over 12,000 feet, most notably Mount Foraker (17,400), Mount Hunter (14,573), Mount Silverthrone (13,220), Mount Crosson (12,772), Kahiltna Dome (12,525), Mount Huntington (12,240), Mount Koven (12,168), and Mount Mather (12,123).

In addition, eight other peaks exceed 10,000 feet within the southern portion of the park. The Alaska Range dates back more than 65 million years, originating from the Denali Fault, which remains the largest crustal break in North America.

In *The Geology of Denali National Park*, Michael Collier asserts that "it's the rare corner of Denali that has not been marked by the passage or presence of ice."[6] Most obvious are the active glaciers that lace the Alaska Range in the southern area of the park. Glaciers are masses of snow, ice, and rock that deform under their own weight and move under the influence of gravity. In an early U.S. Geological Survey, Stephen Capps concluded that in the Denali portion of the Alaska Range, glaciers form on mountains 7,000 feet or more in height, and in general, the size of the glaciers increases with the height of the mountains (although other factors such as exposure to sun and the area of the catchment basins above the permanent snowline are also key).[7] In support of Capps, there are scores of glaciers spawned by Mount McKinley, six of which are from twenty-six to forty-six miles long.[8]

In a later study of "The Glaciation Level in Southern Alaska," Gunnar Ostrom and others concluded that the existence of glaciers within the region was based on several factors, of which winter precipitation, summer temperature, and the length of the melt season are most important.[9] These findings appear to explain the uneven distribution of large glaciers on the south side of the Alaska Range, as compared to the north side. Within the region, the range forms a barrier to the moist air moving up from the Gulf of Alaska, resulting in extensive snowfall on the southern flanks of the range and a precipitation shadow on the north side. In addition, whereas the range divides the interior from the coastal lowlands, summer temperatures are higher in the interior because of the continental effect and significantly milder along the coast due to the moderating effects of water. Consequently, glaciers on the southern side of the range are thicker and longer (see photograph 3.2) than those on the northern slopes, which are smaller and less active.[10] Ruth, Tokositna, Kahiltna, and Eldridge are examples of south-side glaciers, which are from forty to fifty miles long, whereas, on the north side only the Muldrow (about thirty-nine miles in length) is of comparable size.[11]

Of the large glaciers, the Muldrow is the most visible to park visitors, primarily because of its orientation on the north side of the range. The glacier originates beneath an 800-foot icefall on the east flank of Mount McKinley and terminates less than a mile from the road between the Eielson Visitor Center and Wonder Lake.[12] In 1960, Austin Post calculated that the Muldrow covers approximately 152 square miles, winding its way down from the summit snows of Mount McKinley, approximately 39 miles to its terminus at the 2,500-foot elevation level.[13]

It is ironic that although the glacier can be seen and recognized at greater distances from numerous vantage points, many visitors do not recognize its terminus, which rests within a mile of the park road. As Collier explains, "at its terminus, the ice is covered by a two-foot veneer of rock and soil, and supports a plentiful growth of alder and willow."[14] Consequently, the terminus of the Muldrow is often overlooked or mistaken for an area of irregularly shaped tundra.

The Muldrow Glacier has made dramatic surges on two occasions during the past one hundred years, the most recent surge occurring during the winter of 1956-57. One estimate concluded that sections of the Muldrow surged forward as rapidly as 1,100 feet per day before returning to dormancy in 1957.[15] Another study calculated that surface movements of ice amounted to over 6.6 kilometers, and concluded that the surge resulted from unstable dynamic conditions within the glacier system.[16]

Although one may be inclined to think that most of Alaska was previously covered by glaciation because of the state's northerly location, about half of the state was never glaciated. Interestingly, Denali Park lies at the northern edge of the ice-age glaciation that covered much of the northern hemisphere

Photograph 3.2 An aerial view of Tokositna Glacier on the south side of the Alaska range revealing distinct medial and lateral moraines

and retreated between 10,000 and 14,000 years ago (see map 3.1).[17] Indeed, as one travels along the Park Road and passes over the Savage River bridge, the glacial pattern in this northeastern section of the park reveals a stark contrast. To the north of the road, the Savage River has cut a steep V-shaped canyon (see photograph 3.3). To the south of the bridge, however, the land is much less rugged, having been smoothed by glaciers that carved an enormous U-shaped valley through which the Savage River flows (see photograph 3.4).

Throughout most of the park, there are multiple signs of glaciation in addition to the glaciers themselves. Collier explains that in earlier times the Muldrow Glacier had progressed as far north as the Kantishna Hills, beaching a block of ice that

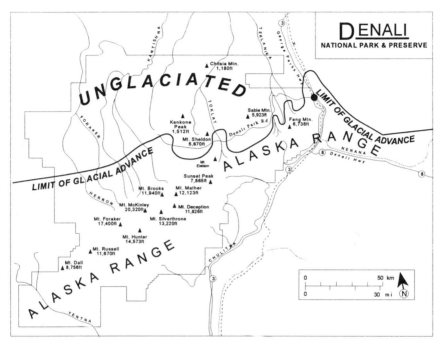

Map 3.1 The northern extent of glaciation in Denali National Park

subsequently formed the cast for "Wonder Lake," twelve miles beyond the glacier's present terminus.[18] Heacox, however, asserts that the Muldrow, passing over a ridge of resistant bedrock, managed to cut a 280-foot-deep gouge into the weaker rock. The cut subsequently filled with water after the glacier retreated and formed the lake that remains today.[19]

Kettle ponds and erratics are other glacial features that appear throughout the park, especially in the lowland areas south of the Park Road. The former were formed by large chunks of ice that broke off from receding glaciers, subsequently melted and formed depressions, and eventually filled with water. The latter are large boulders that were transported along with an advancing glacier and subsequently deposited as the glacier receded. The erratics are fairly obvious because most of these house-size pieces of granite appear to be totally out of context

Photograph 3.3 Looking north from the Savage River bridge at the steep V-shaped, unglaciated canyon cut by the Savage River

within their surrounding landscape (see photograph 3.5). Two excellent examples of the latter can be seen from the park headquarters, resting on the ridge to the immediate south, about thirty miles from where they probably originated. A number of smaller erratics occur in close proximity to the Park Road in the vicinity of Wonder Lake and several near Riley Creek.

Another common glacial feature within the park is the rock glacier; these abound in the northern foothills of the Alaska Range and are visible from the Park Road. This evidence of past glacial activity is particularly evident near Polychrome Pass, where the valleys between the finger-like ridges host piles of rock structured with cores of ice, gradually creeping

Photograph 3.4 Looking south from the same spot as the Savage River flows through an enormous U-shaped valley carved by glaciers

downhill.[20] Other examples are visible south of the Eielson Visitor Center.

Past and present glacial activity impacts virtually all of the fluvial systems within the park. Most rivers and streams are a milky gray color, giving evidence of the glacial debris and ground-up rock that they transport. The major rivers encountered by park visitors originate high in the Alaska Range and drain northward, eventually into the mighty Yukon River, whereas rivers on the south side of the range drain into the Gulf of Alaska. As one travels westward from the park headquarters, the major rivers encountered along the Park Road are, in succession, the Savage, Sanctuary, Teklanika, Toklat

Photograph 3.5 A glacial erratic south of Riley Creek

(including the East and West Branches), Thorofare, and McKinley (see map 3.2). All are glacial and braided. The drainage pattern within Denali is a bit unusual because of the northward orientation of the rivers. The physiography, however, reveals the general slope of the land from the north side of the Alaska Range, gradually descending northward to the Yukon River.

Within Denali, the primary factors that contribute to the braided condition of the rivers are: (1) ice jams in spring and fall, which routinely block channels and detour water along new routes; (2) permafrost areas that inhibit downward erosion and channel deepening; and (3) extremely erratic weather that causes stream volumes to fluctuate widely.[21] These major

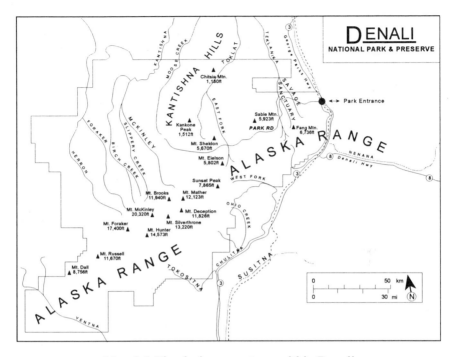

Map 3.2 The drainage pattern within Denali.

rivers are not considered navigable; they are relatively void of fish; and they can be treacherous to cross because of the constantly changing nature of the braids, unpredictable channel depths, and near-freezing water temperatures.

The Teklanika River takes its name from the Athapaskan word meaning "glacier creek," or stream issuing from a glacier.[22] The other rivers share the same heritage, flowing as melt water from the base of glaciers. The Thorofare River is also appropriately named because it acts as a hiker's switchyard, forcing most hikers in this area of the park to eventually cross it because of its migrating nature and countless braids within a two mile channel (see photograph 3.6).[23] The other rivers previously mentioned share these same characteristics, and all continuously transport loads ranging from powdered rock to sand and cobbles.

Clear water streams in the park are relatively few in number and small in size. Tattler Creek in the Sable Pass area and Hogan Creek east of the Sanctuary River are two of the exceptions. Occasionally, one may encounter a clear spring that flows down the side of a mountain.

Another fluvial feature, even less common but readily identifiable, is Horseshoe Lake, an oxbow lake located only about a mile from the visitor access center (see photograph 3.7). Like other oxbows, the lake is a remnant of a river meander that was eventually abandoned via cut-bank erosion within the main channel. Now detached, the lake is located on the west side of the Nenana River and is easily accessible by one of the park's nature trails.

Photograph 3.6 The Thorofare River epitomizes the term "braided river" and poses a continuous challenge to hikers who attempt to cross it.

Climate

The climate of any place shapes the landforms, affects soil composition, determines vegetation types, and influences the type of fauna present. By virtue of its location in the Far North and its position in the interior of Alaska, Denali has a year-round climate that is harsh by almost any visitor's standard. Yet, during the tourist season from June through August, visitors are often surprised by the park's mild weather.

The climate of Denali is dominated by three principal climatic

Photograph 3.7 Horseshoe Lake, a classic oxbow type, located adjacent to the eastern boundary of the park

controls: latitude; the land/water heating differential or "continentality"; and topography, specifically mountain barriers. Latitude has the most significant impact on the climate of the Denali region. The latitudinal position is the distance north or south of the equator and so determines the amount of solar energy received at a given location, with resulting temperatures corresponding to the length of the day and the angle of intensity of the sun. Since the park headquarters is located at about 63 degrees, 45 minutes north, this northerly location receives almost twenty hours of sunlight during the summer solstice, but only about four hours of sun during the winter solstice.[24] Consequently, Denali experiences seasonal extremes in temperatures that peak during the July time frame and bottom out in January. A graph of the average monthly maximum and minimum temperatures for the park reveals the annual pattern (see figure 3.1).

Continentality is the second climatic control that has a significant impact on the climate of the park. The park's interior location places it away from the moderating effects of the oceans and, coupled with the barriers formed by the Alaska Range to the south and the Brooks Range to the north, produces seasonal extremes in temperatures. Figure 3.2 shows the tremendous range between extreme highs and lows and reveals the dramatic range of temperatures throughout the year.

Topography, specifically the mountains of the Alaska Range, provides the third major impact on Denali's climate. The range effectively blocks the moist air flowing north from the Gulf of Alaska, resulting in extensive precipitation on the south (windward) side of the range, but a precipitation shadow on the north (leeward) side. Figure 3.3 graphs the average monthly precipitation for the park.

The previous figures indicate that Denali's summer climate is relatively mild. Visitors should be aware, however, that rain falls on half the days each summer and accounts for most of the annual precipitation recorded at the park headquarters.[25]

Moreover, summer weather conditions can change drastically for the worse in short periods of time, causing temperatures to plummet tens of degrees in less than an hour, fall below freezing, and bring ankle-deep snow in July or knee-deep snow in August.[26] Another unfortunate aspect of the summer climate for visitors is that Mount McKinley (a featured attraction of the park) is normally visible for only 25 to 30 percent of the time. The mountain is routinely visible throughout the long winter, which boasts relatively clear skies in the region. By contrast, the warm, moist summer brings gray skies and clouds that conceal the mountain for extended periods.

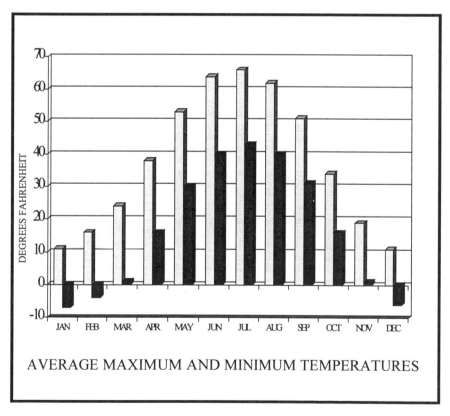

Figure 3.1 Average maximum and minimum monthly temperatures
Source: Alaska Natural History Association, 1994

Snow deserves special attention since up to three feet of it may blanket Denali for six to nine months of the year (see figure 3.4). The low-density, dry, largely recrystallized "taiga snow" of the interior differs significantly from the mountain snow of the western United States in that its temperatures are lower, steeper temperature gradients occur within it, and there is usually much less snowfall.[27] As previously mentioned, however, the snow lasts much longer. Bowling concludes that throughout most of the interior, there is virtually no melting in the snowpack from November until March or April.[28]

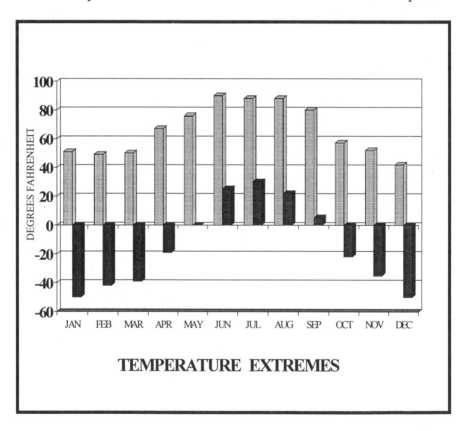

TEMPERATURE EXTREMES

Figure 3.2 Monthly extreme high and low temperatures
Source: Alaska Natural History Association, 1994

Consequently, in most years, it is a major challenge to clear the Park Road all the way to the Eielson Visitor Center prior to the park's opening on Memorial Day weekend.

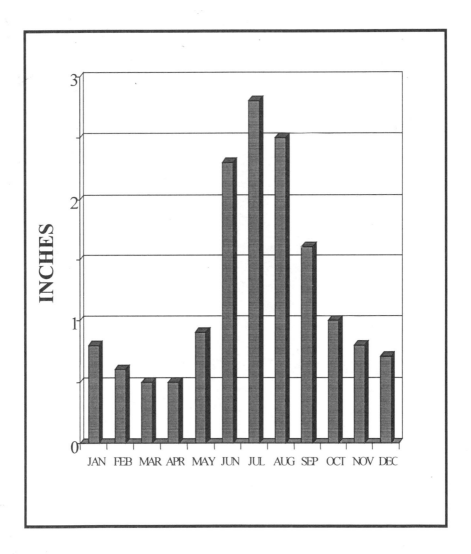

Figure 3.3 Mean monthly precipitation
Source: Alaska Natural History Association, 1999

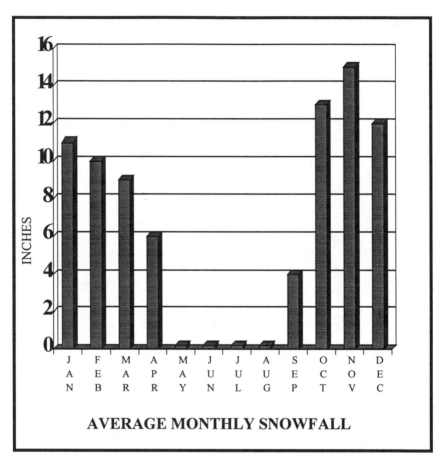

Figure 3.4 Average monthly snowfall
Source: Alaska Natural History Association, 1999

Vegetation

Denali's vegetation is limited by two environmental factors: the severe climate of Alaska's interior and thin layers of top-soil underlain by discontinuous or isolated masses of perma-frost.[29] Although the latter is a result of the former, these two factors nevertheless limit the number of different plant species as well as the relative growth rates of species in the park. Forbes notes that Denali's six million acres host about 750 species of plants, whereas the same size area in Costa Rica can support over 9,000 different plant species.[30] She also concludes that any one of the park's white spruce trees that is seventy-five feet tall can be over 300 years old.[31]

In general, the park consists of two major vegetation regimes: taiga and tundra. The former occurs in the lowland areas of the park, especially in the eastern section. Above the treeline, which is at about 2,700 feet in Denali, taiga gives way to tundra.[32]

Taiga, a Russian word that means "land of little sticks," serves well to describe Denali's stunted and slow-growing forests.[33] Also known as northern boreal forest, taiga endure the largest annual temperature ranges encountered by any of the world's global vegetation regions. Denali's taiga assemblage is dominated by conifers, namely white and black spruce. Tamarack is occasionally found interspersed with black spruce in the flat, boggy northern portion of the park.[34] Deciduous trees are fewer in number but include aspen, balsam poplar, paper birch, and cottonwood.

Throughout interior Alaska, slow-growing black spruce are areally dominant on poorly drained sites, in areas underlain by permafrost, and on north-facing slopes.[35] By contrast, the white spruce are more dominant than black spruce in Denali and prefer much drier soils. Although white and black spruce are not easy to distinguish, the ground cover beneath the former includes a variety of shrubs, herbs, lichens, and berries, whereas the black spruce stands are comprised largely of sphagnum and sedges.[36] Like the trees, the low vegetation reveals a distinctive pattern based on the underlying soil moisture.

One study concludes that the hardwoods of the interior region, particularly paper birch and aspen, occupy sites that are warmer, drier or recently disturbed by fire.[37] Heacox validates the existence of this same pattern in Denali, adding that balsam poplar is also present.[38]

Partial thawing in areas of discontinuous permafrost often creates unique features in the taiga sections of the park. The thawing of upper layers of permafrost in summer is often accompanied by a slippage of soil downslope. This phenomenon, called solifluction, carries along the black spruce trees and causes them to lean in irregular fashions. The unusual pattern created by the spruce trees leaning in various directions is a clear indication of the instability of the underlying soil. Locally, such disturbed areas of spruce are called "drunken forests."[39] Solifluction also occurs in areas of the park above the treeline where the slippage of soil downslope creates lobes of tundra veneer.

Although the timberline is roughly 2,700 feet throughout the park, this limit of tree growth varies according to soil conditions and exposure and may extend up to elevations of 3,500 feet.[40] Beyond the treeline, taiga gives way to tundra, which characterizes most of the park. The change from taiga to tundra is not abrupt, but occurs gradually, revealing an ecotone or transition zone. An ecotone represents a truly different vegetation assemblage prompted by changing conditions in soil, moisture, wind, air temperature, and slope. The result is a transition zone that often contains plant species representing both the taiga and tundra. Moreover, ecotones often prove to be important wildlife habitats because they afford animals multiple opportunities for food and cover (see photograph 3.8).

The tundra of Denali is of two major types: moist and dry. Both types contain a wide variety of shrubs, sedges, mosses, lichens, herbs, and berries. Moist tundra occurs in the lower areas and is characterized by several plant communities, including, willow (of which there are twenty-two varieties), dwarf birch, alder brush, and other waist-high shrubs. At higher elevations the moist tundra transitions into dry or alpine tundra, where winds, cooler temperatures, and thinner soils prevent tundra vegetation from growing above a foot in height. The alpine tundra prevails at elevations above 3,400 feet on exposed mountain ridges and rocky slopes, and ranges up to 7,500 feet.[41] Principal plant species include the eight-petaled avens, net-leaf willow, multiple berries, and a variety of saxi-frages.[42]

River or "gravel" bars are special vegetation assemblages that occur throughout Denali and deserve special mention. Although of lesser significance in terms of areal coverage than the taiga and tundra regimes, the gravel bars provide important wildlife habitats. Prevalent in all of the glacial rivers that flow north out of the Alaska Range, the bars are formed as a result of centuries of shifting channels and gravel deposition and are frequently more than a half-mile wide and tens of miles long.[43]

Photograph 3.8 Moose browsing in the ecotone east of the Savage River camp-ground.

Although plant communities on the bars can be abruptly termi-
nated by floods, ice jams, or channel adjustment, they normally
include a diverse range of vegetation, including alpine hawks-
beard, black oxytrope, dwarf fireweed, and pea vine.[44] In spite
of their semipermanence, gravel bars attract a variety of wildlife in the park, most notably grizzly bears, caribou, and
wolves (see photograph 3.9).

During the course of shuttle bus rides through the park,
visitors routinely expressed interest in three unusual aspects of
the park's vegetation not previously mentioned. The first point
of interest involves a stand of birch and balsam poplar trees
along the Park Road near the hotel (see photograph 3.10). The
trees were badly bowed during an early snowfall in the park

Photograph 3.9 A caribou grazing along a gravel bar

when the weight of the unusually moist, heavy snow was followed by freezing temperatures for an extended period of time. The result of this phenomenon was the unusual pattern of deciduous trees that appear to be bending over.

A second interesting aspect of the vegetation, about which visitors commonly inquire, relates to the brownish triangular growths occurring in some of the spruce trees. Known locally as witches' broom, the growths are a type of fungus common among spruce trees. The growths first become noticeable

Photograph 3.10 Deciduous trees along the Park Road, bent over from the weight of moist, heavy snow and subsequent freezing

among the spruce trees of the ecotone between the park hotel and the Savage River campground but occur elsewhere in the park.

The third unusual aspect of the park's vegetation relates to the stand of spruce trees located on both sides of the Park Road just east of the Toklat River Bridge. Affectionately known as the Porcupine Forest, the area is routinely discussed by the bus drivers. Popular lore suggests that a large number of porcupines were trapped in the area by an early and unusually deep snowfall back in the late 1950s. The porcupines routinely rely on spruce bark as a source of food. The trees occasionally die as a result of extensive girdling. Although not normally noticeable because the girdled trees are spread out over a wider area, the Porcupine Forest stands out because the girdling was concentrated and restricted to the small area for the duration of the winter. The result was a concentration of dead spruce trees that remain more than forty years after the event (see photograph 3.11).

Each of these examples points to unusual aspects of the park's vegetation. Perhaps more importantly, they serve to remind visitors that in Denali, nature should be allowed to do what nature does, and we should be committed to enabling nature to take care of its own.

No discussion of the park's vegetative regime could be complete without mention of the 430 species of wildflowers. All of the species are equally important and all are an integral part of the Denali ecosystem. Nevertheless, the following seem to be particularly popular among bus riders: fireweed, forget-me-nots, bluebells, cotton grass, and squirrel tail grass. Fireweed is common throughout the North Country and is among the first to invade an area after a forest fire. Tall fireweed is also among the first to bloom in the park each year at the start of the tourist season and provides an aethestically pleasing

Photograph 3.11 Porcupine Forest

color to the early season vegetation of the park, especially along the roadsides, dry open areas, and hillsides. Dwarf fireweed also occurs in the park but is generally found in the gravel areas along the rivers. Three types of forget-me-nots are found in the park, the most common of which is the alpine forget-me-not. The latter is also the Alaska state flower and seems to be symbolic in that regard. Bluebells are a more distinguishing aspect of the park and seem to provide a special identity, along with Alaska cotton grass, of which there are several varieties in the park (Alaska, small, and tall cotton grass) and squirrel tail grass. Ironically, the squirrel tail grass, which is so prevalent around the built-up area of the park and perceived to be a distinguishing feature, is an introduced plant and not native to the park.

Aside from the important role they play as an integral part of Denali's ecosystem, wildflowers contribute immeasurably to the park's aesthetic beauty. Visitors are invariably impressed, if not surprised, by the tapestry of colors provided by the hearty flowers of Denali's wild and rugged landscape.

Wildlife

Although they are not normally included in the discussion of a region's physical geography, it is important to mention Denali's large mammals here, as they provided the original justification for the establishment of the park. Moreover, the park's boundaries have been continually adjusted over the years to incorporate the entire range and critical habitats of each of the large mammals. The mammals are an integral part of this intact ecosystem and therefore warrant discussion along with the other major aspects of the park's physical geography. Indeed, one could arguably define Denali as "habitat."

Since the establishment of the park, Denali's wildlife has remained the principal attraction. Bears, caribou, Dall sheep, moose, and wolves have long been the most popular mammals among park visitors.[45] As previously mentioned, the wildlife are completely uninhibited, free to roam anywhere within the park's six million acres and beyond. Consequently, visitors often speculate about their chances of viewing the wildlife, especially since many are accustomed to viewing animals in restricted settings such as in drive-through zoos or nature preserves that ensure controlled animal viewing. Fortunately, the shuttle bus system has proved to be an extremely effective means of assuring visitors the opportunity to view the park's wildlife. A one-week study in July 1988 collected the necessary data to support management decisions related to the shuttle bus service (see figure 3.5).[46] These statistics demonstrate that the shuttle system, which accommodates about forty pairs of eyes aboard each bus, is an effective means of viewing wildlife.

% OF VISITORS REPORTING ANIMAL SIGHTINGS	
BEARS	95%
CARIBOU	95%
DALL SHEEP	95%
MOOSE	82%
WOLVES	24%

Figure 3.5 Animal sightings by shuttle bus passengers

More important, wildlife disturbance has been minimal.

The moose (*Alces alces*) is Denali's largest mammal, with males attaining weights of up to 1,600 pounds. Bulls average between 1,200 and 1,500 pounds, and cows range between 800 and 1,300 pounds (see photograph 3.12). The park's population of about 2,000 moose roam locally between river bottoms and willow patches, covering a twenty- to forty-mile radius.[47] They are frequently found within the ecotones between taiga and tundra, feeding on various types of vegetation. In the spring, Denali moose feed on sedges, grasses, and pond weeds, adding willow, birch, and aspen to their diet in the summer and re-sorting to twigs, bark, and saplings in the winter.[48] Based on an understanding of their diet, one can rightfully conclude that moose are largely concentrated in the taiga and low tundra sections of the eastern and northern areas of the park.

Moose breed in September and October and calves are born from mid-May to early June. A good indication of the health of the range is the presence of twin calves, which may occur from 20 to 50 percent of the time when conditions are favorable. Visitors are usually afforded the opportunity to view newborn calves in the eastern portion of the park throughout the summer months. The newborns are only about thirty pounds at birth and can be well concealed among the willows and alders during their first couple of months; however, they quickly grow to over 300 pounds in a matter of five months.

Like moose, Dall sheep (*Orvis dalli*) are also herbivores. Numbering about 2,500, the sheep are found at higher elevations, inhabiting the rugged high alpine tundra areas of the park, such as the Igloo, Cathedral, and Polychrome Mountain areas. Their ability to inhabit some of the most rugged and inaccessible terrain in the park ensures the Dall sheep protection from predators.

The only species of wild white sheep in the world, Dall sheep generally weigh from 125 to 200 pounds and thrive on flowers, sedges, and grasses in the summer and mosses or lichens during the winter.[49] The sheep are historically important to Denali, in that they were the main attraction that prompted

Photograph 3.12 A bull and a cow moose crossing the park road near the Savage River campground

Charles Sheldon (credited with the founding of the park) to initially travel to the region in 1906 and subsequently lobby to establish a wildlife preserve.

The male sheep, or rams, attain weights of up to 300 pounds and are distinguished by their impressive curling horns. Females are called ewes. They are usually less than 150 pounds and have much shorter, slender, and only slightly curved horns. Lambs are born in late May and early June in the park, usually among the most rugged cliffs of the spring range.

The interior brown bear (*Ursus arctos*), commonly referred to as the grizzly bear, is the most celebrated of Denali's mammals, perhaps because of its symbolic association with pristine wilderness settings. The Denali grizzly is also often referred to as the Toklat grizzly (named after the river system whose abundant gravel bars provide ideal habitats) and is distinguished from other interior brown bears by its light, almost blonde coat (see photograph 3.13). Unlike moose and sheep, the grizzly is omnivorous, with a varied diet that includes 80 to 85 percent vegetation (roots, berries, and grasses) and 15 to 20 percent meat (mainly squirrels and to a lesser degree moose or caribou calves).[50] Because of its reliance upon vegetation, the interior grizzly is much smaller than the coastal brown bear. Whereas the latter may reach heights of over ten feet and attain weights of 1,300 pounds, the former grow to seven feet tall and reach weights of about 700 pounds.

In Denali, grizzlies mate predominantly in May and June and sometimes into early July. Cubs are subsequently born during the hibernation period in midwinter. Most often a sow will have two cubs, which she will continue to nurse for at least two full years and occasionally into the third summer. Visitors frequently observe sows with newborn cubs astride the Park Road anywhere between Sable Pass and the Eielson Visitor Center.

Aldoph Murie studied Denali grizzlies from 1939 to 1970 and concluded that the entire park, except for the upper reaches of the Alaska Range, can be considered grizzly habitat.[51] He also noted seasonal variations in habitat use, such as concentrated activity along gravel bars in the spring, followed by movement into grassy swells such as Sable Pass in the early summer, and a focus on the berry crops of the hillslopes and alpine tundra in late summer and early fall.[52]

Trends from Murie's earlier studies continue to prevail. In his survey between 1961 and 1962, Murie found the greatest concentration of grizzlies to be in the Sable Pass area, with as many as 3.5 to 4.5 bears per square mile. Today, large numbers of bears range between the Toklat and Teklinika Rivers, and Sable Pass (now considered by the National Park Service to be a "critical habitat") continues to be one of the grizzly's favorite areas within the park.

Photograph 3.13 An interior brown bear grazing on a variety of grasses, which, along with roots and berries, account for about 80 percent of its diet

The caribou (*Rangifer tarrandus*) of Denali are migrating animals that cover a much greater range than those previously mentioned. Numbering about 3,200, Denali's herd migrates between summer and winter feeding areas and calving grounds. Like the moose and Dall sheep, caribou are herbivores and feed on willows, grasses, dwarf birch, and succulents in the summer and resort to lichens, mosses, and dried sedges in the winter.[53] Male caribou in the park grow to 400 pounds, while females attain weights of up to 225 pounds. Recent studies have indicated that the herd has been increasing by about 9 percent per year since 1977.[54]

Visitors are often surprised to learn that both the male and female caribou sport antlers. Caribou are in fact the only members of the deer family in which both sexes grow antlers. The rack of a mature bull is significantly larger and more symmetrical, however, than that of a mature female. Interestingly, bulls shed their antlers by early January, whereas females retain theirs during pregnancy until May or June.

The National Park Service considers the presence of wolves (*Canis lupus*) in Denali to be indicative of the quality of the wilderness, and notes that the wolves play important roles as predators within the ecosystem.[55] Wolves help control population size and health by culling old, sick, or newborn caribou, moose, and sheep.[56] The current wolf population is estimated to be about 190, ranging in packs of four to thirty animals.[57] Wolves vary in size and color, with males averaging about 100 pounds and females ranging from 80 to 90 pounds. Much of the current information about Denali's wolves was made available by Adolph Murie in his landmark book, *The Wolves of Mount McKinley*, a classic among wildlife biologists. Murie and present-day biologists conclude that the wolf occupies an important ecological niche in the park.[58]

Two smaller but no less significant mammals that deserve special mention are the hoary marmot (*Marmota caligata*) and the Arctic ground squirrel (*Spermophilus parryi*). The former (one of three species of marmots that inhabit Alaska) resemble large groundhogs and are frequently spotted among the rocky outcrops or talus slops along the Park Road, or even on the road itself, licking salt from the gravel base. The hoary marmots may attain weights of up to ten pounds and are predominantly gray, with a darker back and face and a reddish tail. They are extremely popular among children, who occasionally have the opportunity to watch them up close for an extended period of time.

The Arctic ground squirrel is found throughout the park. Although small in size, the ground squirrel plays an enormous role within the ecosystem. It is at the center of the food web in Denali and is a common source of food for the fox, lynx, wolf, grizzly bear, and golden eagle.

Complementing Denali's fascinating array of mammals are more than 150 species of birds. Many birds are seasonal visitors and travel exceptional distances to arrive at the park. For example, Arctic terns migrate from as far away as Antarctica and the southern extent of South America, and wheateaters range between Denali and Africa. A few of the more commonly recognized species that inhabit the park throughout the year include several different types of grouse (including ruffed, spruce, and sharp-tail), magpie, raven, and gray jay.

Two birds that routinely capture the interest of the shuttle bus riders are the ptarmigan and the mew gull. The former is the Alaska state bird and exists in three varieties in the park: the rock, willow, and white-tailed ptarmigan. The most abundant are the willow ptarmigan which are routinely seen along the Park Road (mainly between mile 5 and the Teklanika campground, and between Eielson and Wonder Lake) where they are attracted to the willow bushes, which are plentiful, and gravel, which aids in digesting their food. Although both males and females are well camouflaged with white plumage during the winter months, one can readily distinguish between the females, which turn entirely brown during the early weeks of summer, and the males, which attain their summer plumage at a slower rate and reveal white feathers among their brown and reddish summer plumage. Bus riders routinely see rock ptarmigan near rocky outcrops at higher elevations. The white-tailed ptarmigan, however, are relatively uncommon in the park.

The mew gull is the other bird that routinely interests visitors, mainly because it is mistaken for a seagull that appears to be far off course, more than 250 miles from the coast. The birds are actually migratory, inhabiting the interior lakes, ponds, and rivers in the spring and summer, and relocating to the coastal areas in late fall. The mew gull is one of three large gulls inhabiting Alaska but is the most common in the Denali region of the interior. Within the park, the mew gulls are frequently found on gravel bars, or near the lakes and ponds.

To the perceptive visitor, animals and animal imprints abound in Denali, reminding us that above all else, Denali is a habitat. Aside from viewing the animal residents, there are numerous other tell-tale signs that reveal the animal/habitat interaction. The following are but a few of the examples that are visible to the perceptive bus rider. Animal trails, particularly those made by caribou and sheep, are routinely visible along the hillsides that parallel the Park Road. Animal tracks, especially bear and caribou, are frequently seen within the soft portions of gravel bars when the shuttle buses cross the park's braided rivers. Snow patches frequently attract caribou throughout the summer months (see photograph 3.14). The latter seek to escape the torment of insects, and snow patches provide clear signs of where the animals had bedded down. Beaver houses are routinely spotted among the kettle ponds in the low tundra areas between Eielson and Wonder Lake. The houses are comprised of tundra veneer and willows and represent an ingenious adaptation in an area that is void of trees, the traditional building material for the beavers. Lastly, one may encounter excavations made by grizzly bears in their attempts to unearth an Arctic ground squirrel. Ironically, the grizzly

Photograph 3.14 Caribou resting on a late-lying snow patch, seeking refuge from the tormenting insects

expends more calories undertaking such an endeavor than it gains from eating the ground squirrel—if it is successful in the effort.

Conclusion

Denali Park's natural landscape is varied, colorful, abundant with wildlife, and even imposing. The multicolored tundra, featuring countless varieties of mosses, lichens, wildflowers, and berries; the dominant mountains of the Alaska Range, laced with glaciers, braided rivers, and streams; and glacial erratics resting upon tundra more than thirty miles from their original sources are only a few of the physical features of the park's natural landscape that promote Denali as a sightseer's paradise. In fact many visitors, as previously mentioned, regard the scenery of this undisturbed subarctic wilderness as the principal attraction.

The widespread perception among visitors is that Denali is a unique national park. Stemming from its location in the Far North, the park's remarkable flora, fauna, and landforms provide scenic opportunities that are not available elsewhere within the national parks system. Perhaps more important, it has felt less of a human impact than any national park in the continental U.S., and the region has survived as one of the largest intact ecosystems in the world.

By understanding some of the unique aspects of the park's physical geography, one can better understand and appreciate many of the visible features that not only comprise the appealing scenery of the park, but serve as distinguishing features of this particular place among other national parks. Recognizing and understanding the unique physical geography of the park also contributes to the preservation of this pristine setting. People not only learn about the unique physical aspects of the place, but they learn to place value on them and to recognize the challenge inherent in managing such a fragile environment. This realization can often result in personal commitment and resolve and serve to supplement one's appreciation of Denali's incomparable physical setting, ultimately contributing to an enduring sense of place.

Notes

1. Rick McIntyre, *Denali National Park: An Island in Time* (Santa Barbara, Calif.: Sequoia Communications, 1986).

2. McIntyre, *Denali National Park.*

3. Alaska Geographic Society, "Denali National Park and Preserve,"

Alaska Geographic 8, no. 4 (1981): 36-37.

4. United States Department of the Interior, National Park Service, *Denali National Park and Preserve*, brochure and map.

5. Clyde Wahrhaftig, "The Alaska Range," *Landscapes of Alaska: Their Geologic Evolution,* ed., Howel Williams (Berkeley: University of California Press, 1958): 48-60.

6. Michael Collier, *The Geology of Denali National Park* (Anchorage: Alaska Natural History Association, 1989), 16.

7. Stephen R. Capps, *The Kantishna Region, Alaska, USGS Bulletin 687* (Washington, D.C.: Government Printing Office, 1919).

8. Elaine Rhode, "Denali Country," *Alaska Geographic* 15, no. 3 (1988): 6-21. A quick glance at the widely sold LANDSAT image of the Denali National Park area clearly reveals the significant increase in glacial activity on the south side of the Alaska Range. The image is sold in poster format in various bookstores or can be ordered directly from the U.S. Geological Survey.

9. Gunnar G. Ostrom, N. Haakensen, and T. Eriksson, "The Glaciation Level in Southern Alaska," *Geografiska Annaler* 63A, nos. 3-4 (1981): 251-260.

10. Steve Buskirk, *Denali: The Story behind the Scenery* (Las Vegas: KC Publications, 1989). A quick look at any of the USGS maps of the Denali region reveals the vivid contrast between the size and length of south slope versus north slope glaciers.

11. Wahrhaftig, "The Alaska Range."

12. Kim Heacox, *The Denali Road Guide* (Denali National Park: Alaska Natural History Association, 1986).

13. Austin Post, "The Exceptional Advances of the Muldrow, Black Rapids, and Susitna Glaciers," *Journal of Geophysical Research* 65, no. 11 (1960): 3703-3712.

14. Collier, *The Geology of Denali National Park*, 17.

15. Collier, *The Geology of Denali National Park*, 17.

16. Post, "The Exceptional Advances of the Muldrow."

17. Buskirk, *Denali*. See also Wahrhaftig, "The Alaska Range"; Collier, *The Geology of Denali National Park*; and Ostrom et al., "The Glaciation Level in Southern Alaska."

18. Collier, *The Geology of Denali National Park*, 17.

19. Heacox, *The Denali Road Guide*.

20. Collier, *The Geology of Denali National Park*.

21. Heacox, *The Denali Road Guide*.

22. Heacox, *The Denali Road Guide*.

23. Collier, *The Geology of Denali National Park*.

24. Sue Ann Bowling, "The Weather and Climate of Alaska," *Weatherwise* 33, no. 5 (1980): 196-201.

25. Heacox, *The Denali Road Guide*.

26. Heacox, *The Denali Road Guide*.

27. Carl S. Benson, "Alaska's Snow," *Weatherwise* 33, no. 5 (1980): 202-206.

28. Bowling, "The Weather and Climate of Alaska."

29. Jesse Ford and Barbara L. Bedford, "The Hydrology of Alaskan Wetlands, USA: A Review," *Arctic and Alpine Research* 19, no. 3 (1987): 209-229. A casual glance at the cut banks along the Park Road provides a cross-section of the tundra veneer and reveals the thin layer of topsoil.

30. Sheri Forbes, *The Nature of Denali* (Denali National Park: Alaska Natural History Association, 1992), 15.

31. Forbes, *The Nature of Denali*, 15.

32. United States Department of the Interior, National Park Service, *Denali National Park and Preserve*, brochure and map. Variations also occur based on soil composition, and whether a given slope is north facing or south facing.

33. McIntyre, *Denali National Park*.

34. Buskirk, *Denali*.

35. D. F. Grigal, "Extractable Soil Nutrients and Permafrost under Adjacent Forest Types in Interior Alaska," *Northwest Science* 53, no. 1 (1979): 43-50.

36. Buskirk, *Denali*. Generally, the white spruce is a much fuller and healthier-looking tree than the black spruce.

37. Grigal, "Extractable Soil Nutrients and Permafrost."

38. Heacox, *The Denali Road Guide*.

39. Heacox, *The Denali Road Guide*. The shuttle bus drivers routinely point out examples along the Park Road.

40. Adolph Murie, *Mammals of Denali*, 5th ed. (Anchorage: Alaska Natural History Association, 1983).

41. Buskirk, *Denali*.

42. Buskirk, *Denali*.

43. Buskirk, *Denali*.

44. Buskirk, *Denali*.

45. Charlie Loeb, "Wildlife from the Bus Window," *Denali Alpenglow* Vol. 14 (Summer 1992): 7.

46. Loeb, "Wildlife from the Bus Window," 7.

47. Kim Heacox, *In Denali* (Santa Barbara, Calif.: Jane Freeburg, 1992).

48. Heacox, *In Denali*.

49. Heacox, *The Denali Road Guide*; and *In Denali*.

50. Heacox, *In Denali*.

51. Adolph Murie, *The Grizzlies of Mount McKinley*, United States Department of Interior, National Parks Service, Scientific Monograph Series no. 14 (Washington, D.C.: Government Printing Office, 1981).

52. Murie, *The Grizzlies of Mount McKinley*.

53. Heacox, *In Denali*.

54. Heacox, *In Denali*.

55. United States Department of the Interior, National Park Service, *Denali National Park and Preserve*, brochure and map.

56. United States Department of the Interior, brochure and map.

57. Heacox, *In Denali*.

58. Heacox, *The Denali Road Guide*.

4

Cultural Geography

A common distinction between cultural and physical geography is that the former refers to the study of culture patterns, while the latter focuses on patterns created by the physical processes on the earth.[1] The physical geography of Denali describes the physical component of the place, evolving independently of human activity and providing a setting for human experience. The third of the integral components of place, the cultural aspect, is approached here through describing the evolving cultural imprint in Denali (a clearly visible artifact) and seeking to understand the "meaning" that visitors impart to the place (a cultural dimension that is not so apparent). Like many humanist cultural geographers, I seek to explain the nature of place through a physical geographic analysis but hope to understand humans, social interactions, and individual behavior (within the context of Denali) through the use of cultural geography.[2]

The cultural component of a place includes human activities and processes, their resulting material imprint, and the ideas people bring with them, formulate, and take away when they depart. The meanings that people impart to a place are just as important to the distinction of that place as the material culture, which supplements the physical landscape to form a visible and durable imprint. As such, I examine the cultural component of Denali National Park from two perspectives that I believe to be complementary: traditional cultural geography and the "new" cultural geography. While the former emphasizes the cultural residual on the landscape, the latter acknowledges the significance of the inner workings of culture and seeks to "reveal the underlying forces that condition human behavior, especially those affecting human relations with the physical environment."[3] Both perspectives are necessary to understand the cultural component of Denali.

The Traditional Legacy

Cultural geography is regarded as "a subfield of human geography that focuses upon the patterns and interactions of human culture, both material and non-material, in relation to the natural environment."[4] From a traditional perspective, the cultural component of Denali focuses on the relationships between people and their environment and the resulting cultural landscape. To clarify, "people" includes visitors to the park as well as seasonal employees and year-round residents; while the cultural landscape is conceptualized as the human imprint on the natural environment, the visible, material residual of human activities and processes.

One can approach the study of cultural geography by focusing either on human activities or on the product of those activities, that is, the material culture and cultural landscape.[5] In either case, "the behavior produces the material culture, and the material culture is the product of the behavior."[6] Based on this logic, I use both approaches to examine the cultural component of Denali and ultimately to explain the cultural patterns that prevail.

Cultural Landscape

In 1925, Carl Sauer identified a logical progression that natural landscapes undergo as they are affected by human and natural processes over time. He asserted that cultures as agents transform the natural landscape into a cultural landscape and specifically noted that "culture is the agent, the natural area is the medium, the cultural landscape the result."[7]

Later interpretations of Sauer's seminal statement observed that by studying the cultural landscape, geographers could learn about the previous and present occupants, since the cultural landscape reflects the way of life of the inhabitants. Arguably, one can learn an equal amount about an area based on what is not present in the cultural landscape, and/or the degree to which the natural landscape has been transformed into a cultural landscape. Such is the case with Denali National Park, which reveals only a subtle cultural imprint despite having been visited by millions of people over many decades.

The evolution of the cultural landscape of Denali can be viewed as a continuum, evolving gradually over the past eighty years. As previously explained in the historical chapter, permanent settlements never occurred within the present-day boundaries of the park, and seasonal hunters did not leave an enduring imprint. Consequently, the cultural landscape did not begin to evolve until the formal establishment of the park in 1917. Developments since have been carefully planned and scrutinized by the National Park Service.

The most well developed portion of Denali's cultural landscape is contained within the small built-up area just inside the entrance to the park. As previously noted, the area comprises less than 0.1 percent of the total acreage of the park. The zone functions as the reception and host area for visitors to the park and performs certain educational and administrative purposes as well. The area houses the park's permanent residents, park offices, and administrative buildings (see photograph 4.1) and features the park hotel, the railroad depot (see photograph 4.2), and the visitor access center (see photograph 4.3). These facilities are linked by a simple road network and a number of nature trails.

Outside of the built-up area, the human imprint is less conspicuous. The Park Road is the dominant feature and extends from the entrance of the park to the Wonder Lake ranger station, a distance of about ninety miles. The road is a primitive, gravel surface that follows the lay of the land and provides access to the park via the shuttle bus system. Since shuttle bus riders focus their attention out of the bus windows, this cultural feature, which contrasts sharply with the wilderness surroundings, is not as noticeable to the average visitor (at least during the bus ride) as one might expect.

Along the Park Road a number of bridges have been constructed to permit passage across the numerous braided rivers. The bridges are all of a simple design and do not obstruct the view of the tourists as the latter cross aboard the shuttle buses (see photograph 4.4). The bridges are regarded merely as an extension of the Park Road, and so they do not warrant special attention.

Inasmuch as the overwhelming percentage of the park's cultural landscape appears within the road corridor, I have identified three classes of features that are prevalent in this segment of the park and warrant special attention: rest stops, campgrounds, and ranger stations. Each of these classes is readily identifiable, performs a specific function, and serves as a setting for interaction.

Rest Stops

The most noticeable features along the Park Road are the rest stops, situated at the Teklanika River, Polychrome Pass, the

Photograph 4.1 The park headquarters and superintendent's office

Toklat River, Eielson, and Wonder Lake. As one travels westward into the park after boarding the shuttle bus at the visitor access center, rest stops are made at Teklanika River, Polychrome Pass, Eielson, and Wonder Lake. The return trip eastward includes stops at Eielson, Toklat River, and Teklanika River, before arriving back at the visitor center. The rest stops are worthy of special attention because they provide the settings where the overwhelming majority of park visitors form the most intimate relationships with the wilderness surroundings.

The rest stops serve as focal points for the visitor experience. They provide the opportunity for close encounters with nature and/or fellow bus riders. Moreover, the rest stops are nodes where the activity spaces of all shuttle bus riders

Photograph 4.2 The railroad depot, a key link to the park

converge, and thus serve as points for social interaction, mutual reinforcement of experience, and development of consensus images of the place (see photograph 4.5). I discovered that at the end of their day's journey aboard the shuttle bus, many tourists best described their memory of the Denali experience as a collage of images formed at the various rest stops.

The first rest stop during the westward trip along the Park Road occurs at approximately mile 30 along the Teklanika River. Teklanika is an Athapaskan word that means "stream issuing from a glacier" and is an appropriate name for this braided river. The rest stop normally occurs about one hour and ten minutes after departing the visitor access center. The stop is best described as a gravel turnout along the road and

Photograph 4.3 The visitor access center

includes a number of portable toilets and an interpretative display overlooking the river. The orientation of the tourists' view is toward the west and northwest, across the braided river into a spruce forest on the far side. Caribou are the most commonly observed form of wildlife in this area and are usually seen traveling along the gravel bars. Up to this point in the trip along the Park Road, visitors saw nature through the bus windows. The Teklanika rest stop, however, affords the first opportunity for bus riders to develop a more intimate relationship with the natural surroundings. People get off the bus, walk around, and smell, hear, and touch the nature of Denali. Although noticeably timid at first, visitors are filled with anticipation and reveal a distinct curiosity and appreciation of the wilderness, yet appear somewhat relieved to experience the latter from within the security of the group. This typical reaction suggests that "wilderness" is very much a function of one's perception.

The second rest stop during the westward trek along the Park Road occurs at Polychrome Pass, located at about mile 46, about two hours and forty-five minutes travel time from the visitor center. Polychrome is an appropriate name for the multicolored rock, strata, and talus slopes of the area. The rest stop is more elaborate than the Teklanika stop and includes several interpretative displays, permanent toilet facilities housed in a rustic building, and a nature trail that traverses the high alpine

Photograph 4.4 A bridge spanning the Teklanika River is typical of the dozen or so bridges that enable the Park Road to span the north-flowing braided rivers along its ninety-mile course.

Photograph 4.5 Bus riders sharing their enthusiasm while stopping for an opportune photograph

tundra (see photograph 4.6). The dominant view is toward the south, where a breathtaking panorama includes the Alaska Range, several distinct glaciers, a number of house-sized glacial erratics, kettle ponds, and a number of braided rivers (see photograph 4.7). Tourists spend a considerable amount of their allotted time trying to capture the scenery from this particular vantage point in the park. The tundra walk provides an opportunity to feel the soft, cushion-like, but fragile high alpine tundra beneath one's feet, and observe an assortment of wildflowers amid the ever-present cool and crisp breeze at about the 3,700 foot elevation mark. Wildlife commonly seen from the Polychrome rest stop include caribou walking along the gravel

Photograph 4.6 Visitor facilities at Polychrome rest stop

bars of the braided rivers to the south, marmots among the rocky outcrops throughout the rest area, golden eagles soaring above, Dall sheep grazing in the hills to the north and east, and an occasional grizzly bear to the north or west. Polychrome Pass is extremely diverse and scenic from any perspective, and strongly encourages group interaction that usually continues as people reboard the buses (see photograph 4.8).

The third rest stop along the westbound trip occurs at the Eielson Visitor Center, located at mile 66, approximately three hours and forty-five minutes travel time from the visitor access center. The Eielson Visitors' Center is by far the most elabo-rate built structure west of the Savage River (see photo-

Photograph 4.7 A view looking south from Polychrome rest stop

graph 4.9). The facility includes restrooms, a small gift shop, a viewing platform, several picnic tables, and a host of interpretative displays and maps.

The rest stop encourages interaction by providing a nature trail that winds through the high alpine tundra of the area. The facility is named after Alaska's pioneer bush pilot, Carl Ben Eielson. Throughout the duration of the rest stop most people focus their attention toward the southwest, where the summit of Mount McKinley is located approximately 33 miles distant, close enough, however, to fill the lens of most cameras. The visitor center is situated on a bluff overlooking the Thorofare

River, with the Muldrow, Sunset, and West Fork glaciers plainly visible and the Mount McKinley massif dominating the view.

Caribou abound in this area of the park during the tourist season, and visitors routinely see grizzly bears just to the east of the rest stop, hoary marmots in the immediate vicinity, and golden eagles flying above Mount Galen and Thorofare Mountain to the north. Like the Polychrome rest stop, the site at Eielson offers visitors abundant wildlife, a variety of landforms, and colorful wildflowers. The majestic scenery and cool breeze encourage visitors to relax, share the experience, and try to capture as much of the setting as possible by looking and thinking or by taking photographs.

Photograph 4.8 Developing community spirit, bus riders congregating and enjoying the view from Polychrome rest stop

Half of all the shuttle bus excursions into the park have Eielson as their destination, and hence begin the return trip back to the visitor access center after the rest stop. The other half of the excursions continue their westward trek toward Wonder Lake. The Wonder Lake rest stop is located at mile 86, a five-hour-and-twenty-five-minute bus ride from the start point, and the turnaround point for the longer excursion into the park. The rest stop enables visitors to get out and explore Wonder Lake or remain in the vicinity of the campground, which commands a majestic view of Mount McKinley. Moose are commonly seen in the vicinity, as are caribou. Low tundra and numerous kettle ponds dominate the area. The most coveted views and photographs are focused south across the low tundra and McKinley River toward the north face of Mount McKinley.

To the delight of the bus riders, the first stop on the return trip from Wonder Lake includes a stop at the Eielson Visitor Center, affording visitors a second chance to get a glimpse of "the high one," which is routinely shrouded in clouds about 70 percent of the time. Additionally, passengers have the opportunity to take advantage of the superb interpretative displays, hike south toward the edge of the bluff overlooking the Thorofare River, or briefly explore Thorofare Mountain to the immediate north of Eielson. All of these latter options are normally sacrificed during the first stop at Eielson in order to acquire photographs and/or bask in the warm sun atop the breezy bluff, gazing at Denali or visually searching for wildlife.

The second rest stop (or the first if Eielson, as opposed to Wonder Lake, was the destination) along the return trip eastward occurs along the west bank of the Toklat River at approximately mile 53. The buses are able to park only a few feet from the north-flowing Toklat, thanks to the gravel outwash of this braided river. Facilities at the rest stop include a half-dozen portable toilets, a couple of picnic tables, and most notably two bronze plaques paying tribute to Charles Sheldon the

Photograph 4.9 Looking eastward towards Eielson Visitor Center

founder of Denali, and Harry Karstens, Sheldon's guide and the park's first superintendent. Because of the location on the gravel bar, the Toklat River rest stop does not restrict the visitor's focus to a single cardinal direction. Scenic beauty and possibilities for spotting wildlife exist in all directions. Caribou are frequently seen walking along the gravel bars of the river in the foreground to the north, east, and south. Grizzly bears are also routinely observed along the gravel bars, as well as on the side of the hill to the immediate west of the rest stop. An almost sure bet, however, is to look due east and observe bands of Dall sheep grazing in the grassy swales of the western edge of the Polychrome Mountain massif overlooking the east bank of the Toklat. Although the rest stop is of shorter duration than those at Eielson or Wonder Lake, the stop at Toklat enables visitors to visually experience a sizable areal extent, to walk along the gravel bars, to hear and touch the cold, fast-flowing glacial waters of the Toklat, and to marvel at Divide Mountain to the southeast, Polychrome Mountain to the east, and Cabin Peak and Mount Sheldon to the north.

The final rest stop along the return trip for all excursions occurs at the Teklanika River. In contrast to the atmosphere at all other rest stops, this last stop at Teklanika is characterized more by the desire to use the toilets, stretch the legs, and engage in conversation to review the day's events than to experience the nature of Denali. Whereas the initial stop at Teklanika reveals visitors filled with anticipation, milling about in a timid fashion and trying to figure out how to look at what's out there, this final stop features tourists who feel more like insiders than outsiders and are eager to return to the visitor access center to tell other curious yet inexperienced visitors (still regarded as outsiders) about the excursion.

Campgrounds

Denali boasts seven campgrounds, three of which are only accessible via the shuttle bus system. Collectively, the campgrounds can accommodate 291 campers. They are notable not only for their contribution to Denali's sparsely developed cultural landscape, but also because they serve as focal points for interaction among visitors to the park and because they attract a different category of visitor than those who simply experience Denali aboard the shuttle bus. Whereas some shuttle bus riders have limited physical mobility (mainly because of age), campers tend to be in better physical condition (except for those at the sites permitting recreational vehicles), and thus have the capacity to seek solitude and develop what they perceive as a more personal encounter with nature. The latter use the campground as a base of operation from which to hike about and explore each day. Nevertheless, the campers use the campsites just as the bus riders use the rest stops, as settings for social interaction. Here again, visitors seek mutual reassurance and give credibility to one another's experience. Interestingly, campers feel that they are more bona fide insiders than those who simply ride the shuttle bus and that their more intimate experience with the wilderness is more authentic.

Of the seven campgrounds, two are located east of the Savage River, in proximity to the built-up area of the park. The Riley Creek campground is located just inside the entrance to the park, approximately one-quarter of a mile west of the Parks Highway and on the south side of the Denali Park Road. Riley Creek is the only campground in the park open all year. The campground has 100 sites for tents and RVs and includes water, a flush toilet, and a sewage dump station. This campground is the most accessible and is located in close proximity to all facilities in the built-up area of the park. Daily interpretative programs are featured during the summer months.

The Savage River campground is located at mile 13.3 along the south side of the Park Road. The campground has thirty-three sites for RVs and tents and includes water and a flush toilet. As at Riley Creek, daily interpretative programs are featured during the summer months. Because Savage River is comfortably separated from the built-up section of the park, visitors perceive that it provides more of a wilderness feeling than the Riley Creek campground.

The Sanctuary River campground is located at mile 23 along the Park Road. This campground is a more primitive facility, featuring seven sites for tents only. There are neither water sources nor interpretative programs, and open fires are not permitted; however, a chemical toilet is provided. Campers at the Sanctuary River campground tend to be younger hiking enthusiasts who usually seek to acquire a seat aboard the shuttle bus each day, flagging down a westbound shuttle bus in order to be transported to another location along the Park Road to conduct a day hike. Later, they flag down an eastbound shuttle bus and return to the campground to spend the night.

The Teklanika River campground is located at mile 29 along the Park Road, and is the only one of the four campgrounds west of the Savage River that permits RVs. The campground has fifty-three sites for RVs and tents and offers a water source, a chemical toilet, and daily interpretative programs for campers. Vehicle campers are required to stay for a minimum of three nights in order to minimize turbulence within the campground and traffic along the Park Road. Campers at this location tend to be older and less mobile than those at all other campgrounds west of the Savage River.

The Igloo Creek campground is more primitive than the Teklanika site and is comparable to the Sanctuary River campground. Igloo Creek accommodates tents only at its seven sites and is located at mile 34 along the Park Road. Like the Sanctuary River campground, Igloo Creek has neither water nor interpretative programs and does not permit open fires. Whereas the former boasts a chemical toilet, the latter has a pit toilet. Like those at Sanctuary River, campers here tend to be active hikers and/or use the shuttle bus system daily and conduct day hikes in other areas, returning nightly to the campground.

From the perspective of many campers, the Wonder Lake campground is the ultimate camping experience in Denali because of its location at the end of the Park Road at mile 85 in the heart of Denali, and the majestic view of Mount McKinley only twenty-seven miles distant. The Wonder Lake campground has twenty-eight sites for tents only, water, flush toilets, and frequently scheduled interpretative programs. No open fires are permitted, and the ever-present mosquitoes at this location are certain to gain the attention of the campers. Nevertheless, the vantage point offered by this campground enables one to look out tens of miles across the gently rolling low tundra into the north side of the Mount McKinley massif, a view that is spectacular yet different each hour of the day.

Ranger Stations

The ranger stations in the park are best described as large sin-
gle-room log structures. They were all constructed during the
1920s and 1930s and were initially positioned to be about a
one-day journey by sled dogs. As expected, the rustic cabins
have been well maintained by the National Park Service and
blend in well with their natural surroundings. Nevertheless, the
ranger stations are noteworthy since they are the only built
forms that appear along the Park Road, aside from the rest stop
facilities and bridges. Moreover, the ranger stations are symbolic in that they provide a feeling of security to travelers
journeying through the wilderness.

As one travels west along the Park Road, the first ranger
cabin occurs at mile 22.7. Built in the 1920s, the structure is
positioned on the south side of the road and along the Sanctuary River. As one continues west, the next ranger station is encountered at mile 34.1 (see photograph 4.10), positioned on the
north side of the road and along Igloo Creek. The third cabin
along the westward excursion is located at mile 42.9. Previously known as Adolph Murie's cabin, the East Fork ranger
station is situated south of the road and overlooks the East
Fork River. After crossing the long bridge over the Toklat
River, one encounters the Toklat ranger station at approximately mile 53 (see photograph 4.11). The cabin is nestled at
the base of a 6,200-foot mountain and looks south across the
Toklat River at Divide Mountain and northeast to Polychrome
Mountain. Since the Eielson Visitor Center, located at mile 66,
serves as a ranger station, the fifth cabin is not encountered
until one reaches mile 86.7 in the vicinity of Wonder Lake.
The Wonder Lake ranger station was built in the 1930s and
oversees activities at the campground, as well as controlling
the western terminus of the Park Road.

The ranger stations, along with the campgrounds and rest
stops, comprise the visible cultural imprint along the road corridor through the park. Each of the features performs a par-

ticular function and each provides a setting for interaction. Visitors conclude that the human impact in the park is limited to these classes of features, in addition to the Park Road. The features are significant in that while they blend in well with the natural surroundings, they enable visitors to experience the wilderness with a sense of security. Together they constitute only a small percentage of the vast acreage of Denali. Nevertheless, they represent ways in which people have signified themselves on the natural landscape.

In the traditional sense, the cultural material residual of the cultural landscape and the extent of development tells us much about the people who occupied the area. Similarly, the underdeveloped cultural landscape of the park serves to remind us of

Photograph 4.10 The Igloo Creek ranger cabin at mile 34.1

Photograph 4.11 The Toklat ranger station, at mile 53.1

the inhospitable and inaccessible nature of the place for much of its history. It also suggests, however, that a harmonious relationship has existed between occupying groups, however brief, and the natural environment. Moreover, it demonstrates the conscious effort on the part of the National Park Service to minimize the human imprint in this pristine wilderness setting and to carefully plan, site, and construct only those few forms that are deemed necessary.

Cultural Activities

One can never fully understand a place by simply describing its physical attributes, regardless of whether they are of natural or cultural origin. Understanding can come about only after considering the activities, moods, expectations, and perceptions of the people experiencing the place.

In order to establish a link between the cultural landscape and culture, it seems logical to initially focus on the cultural landscape, the imprint on the natural landscape that results from cultural activities. Subsequent emphasis is placed on human interactions with the environment and addresses those activities that create the cultural landscape. Two key concepts relative to this approach include sense of place, and spirit of place. The former may be regarded as "the particular experience of a person in a particular setting"; and the latter as "the combination of characteristics that gives some locations a special feel or personality."[8] Both concepts are important in better comprehending the nature of the Denali experience, and both enhance understanding of the place.

By shifting the focus from the cultural landscape of Denali to the visitor culture, one can better assess the meanings that people impart to the place as well as the impact that Denali has on them. In this vein, the specificity of Denali has been associated with the unique experiences people have in the place and the meanings that they associate with those experiences.[9] A better understanding of the cultural activities undertaken in Denali may illuminate some of the distinguishing aspects of the place that are not recorded in the cultural landscape.

Sightseeing is the primary visitor activity in Denali National Park. Fishing, boating, hunting, picnicking, bicycling, hiking, camping, mountain climbing, and other activities so prevalent in other national parks account for only a small percentage of visitor use hours in Denali. The quest to experience the wilderness by sightseeing may take several forms: camping, hiking, or riding aboard the park's shuttle bus. As one might expect, perspectives of the Denali experience differ among these different categories of visitors. Indeed, my interviews with people from each category revealed their distinct preference for being associated with and recognized as a member of a particular subset of park visitors.

Hikers claimed to have the most intimate experience in the park based on their ability to explore the wilderness at their own pace, find solitude, and cultivate a personal relationship with nature. Campers recognize the intimate experience gained by hikers, but also perceive that their own activity enables them to develop an intimate relationship with the nature of the park, at least more so than by simply riding the shuttle bus. Campers admit that hikers may cover more ground, but insist that the hiker's experience is no more intense than their own. Both hikers and campers perceive the shuttle bus riders to be too far removed from the nature of the park to have a truly intimate encounter, unless the latter occasionally get off the bus and experience the park on a more individual basis. Ironically, the bus riders perceive their own experience to be no less authentic than those of the hikers and campers, despite developing their sense of place based on social interaction aboard the bus and at the rest stops, viewing the wilderness through the bus windows, and acquiring a more heightened experience only at specific vantage points along the Park Road.

Mutual reinforcement and legitimacy are important concepts affecting the bus riders' experience. It seems that the bus riders benefit from covering a maximum amount of territory in the park, and further benefit from the social aspects of sharing information with other riders and mutually reinforcing the authenticity of the experience. They have the opportunity to develop consensus images of the park from a greater number and diversity of locations, and with forty pairs of eyes instead of one or two, they believe that they acquire a greater breadth of knowledge of the place. Moreover, the opportunity to verify and accentuate what was seen along the excursion at subsequent rest stops seems to contribute to an enduring sense of place.

All of the above categories of visitors arrive at the park with different backgrounds and interests, and subsequently undertake different activities. Consequently, their sense of place is bound to be different from both a personal and a group perspective. Nevertheless, a commonality among all individuals is that their wilderness encounter is perceived to be personal and authentic, and the spirit of the place has an undeniable and enduring impact on their experience.

Since the shuttle bus riders account for a disproportionate number of visitors to the park, I have focused on trying to understand the nature of their experience as it contributes to a place geography of Denali. The following account serves to capture the insights of the shuttle bus riders and to illuminate what visitors perceive as the spirit of the place.

Perspectives from Shuttle Bus Riders

I sought to better understand the experience of the shuttle bus riders through participant observation and by administering a questionnaire and conducting informal interviews during the summers of 1993 and 1994. I synthesized the perspectives from the completed questionnaires in order to incorporate various aspects of the bus riders' experience as it contributes to the cultural component of Denali.

The 1993 questionnaire was designed to: (1) unveil some of the general reasons people visit the park; (2) discover what they find attractive about the natural setting; (3) examine personal feelings they develop toward the place; (4) identify what they perceive to be unique about the park; and (5) establish whether they regarded their experience as therapeutic. All of the questionnaires and interviews were administered during daily shuttle bus excursions into the park. The following findings summarize the responses to the questions posed in several hundred completed questionnaires and dozens of informal interviews conducted at Denali National Park over a two-year period.

The overwhelming majority of the respondents were making their first visit to Denali National Park. Reasons for visiting the park can be grouped into the following general explanations. (1) "I wanted to get away from it all." (2) "I was attracted to Denali because of its reputation as an undisturbed natural setting in a frontier area." (3) "I wanted to experience the excitement of a distant and unusual place." (4) "I simply wanted to see it." These responses indicate that distance, remoteness, and the uniqueness of a pristine natural setting appear to be key factors that attract visitors to the park.

In general, all park visitors were greatly impressed by and strongly attracted to the natural setting. Visitors indicated that the visual aspects of the place were among the most appealing features. Those aspects of the natural setting that were regarded as aesthetically pleasing were most popular. Particular mention was made of the scenery, mountains, sunsets, and streams and rivers. Another appealing feature is the perceived authenticity of the natural setting. In this regard, people were convinced by the lack of human imprint, the varied and abundant wildlife, and the clean air.

Personal sentiments toward the place indicated that most people were convinced of an authentic encounter with nature, where the pristine setting prompted a mental and physical response. Typical feelings included the following. (1) "The place made me feel small." (2) "I felt very refreshed." (3) "The place made me think a lot." (4) "Don't ever change this place."

In describing their personal feelings, individuals did not appear to be biased by any stories or myths about Denali. Prior to their visit, most tourists were completely unaware of any Athapaskan history or philosophy related to the park, Mount McKinley, or the environs.

One might expect, given the "pre-selected" nature of most park visitors, that many tourists would have encountered aspects of the park that were already familiar in the context of their life experience. Visitors were nearly unanimous, however, in declaring that "nothing" about the place seemed familiar. This response emphasizes the uniqueness or specificity of the place. On the other hand, people noted that "almost everything" about Denali seemed to be unique. Among the most distinguishing characteristics they noted were that it was vast, untouched, wild, undisturbed, quiet, and lacked any distractions. It appears that these defining characteristics enabled most visitors to have an intense experience, form a clear mental picture, gain a lasting impression, and develop a strong sense of place.

Inasmuch as most tourists develop various preliminary hopes and aspirations regarding their destinations, it was important to inquire about the feelings that visitors expected to have about this place before they arrived. Typical responses revealed that visitors anticipated excitement, adventure, great scenery, and symbolic wildlife. Many indicated that they were "not sure what to expect, but were certain that it would be great." These responses indicate that all visitors had great expectations, and all had prejudged the place in a positive light.

In response to queries about whether their expectations had been fulfilled, most visitors described a tremendous sense of fulfillment that had exceeded their expectations by any measure. Most declared that they "had never seen nor experienced any place like Denali." Moreover, visitors were convinced of an "authentic" rather than a "contrived" experience.

An intriguing aspect of the visitor experience was the general contention that most people felt better, physically, mentally, spiritually, or some combination thereof, after visiting the park. In fact, most visitors claimed to have "felt better in all respects." The following statements expressed typical sentiments. "I felt refreshed." "I relaxed, felt good about what I saw, and enjoyed the chance to just look and think." "I appreciated the natural grandeur." A commonality among these and many other descriptions is the emphasis on the positive and personal nature of the place encounter.

Most visitors concluded that there are therapeutic or healing aspects associated with this place; however, most chose to describe rather than explain their assertions. The following are typical examples. "The place provided a closeness with nature." "Denali is peaceful, harmonious, and relaxing." "I felt contentment." "I had more energy." "I was able to recharge my batteries." In all cases, individuals described Denali as a "place of health" that had a positive impact on them.

Unanticipated yet convincing survey and interview responses relating to the therapeutic nature of the Denali experience prompted more detailed investigation into this matter during the following summer. Specific objectives were to: (1) place the visitor perspectives of Denali within a larger context by revealing the scope of the visitors' previous experience and by asking them to compare Denali to other national parks; (2) gain more insight into the motivations for visiting the place; (3) recognize which features of the natural setting contribute to the enduring sense of place; (4) re-examine the distinguishing aspects of the place; and (5) assess the visitor commitment to maintaining the place as it is for use by future generations. The following discussion integrates and synthesizes the results of questionnaires and interviews that were administered during fieldwork conducted in the park during the summer of 1994.

Suspecting that most park visitors were well traveled and frequented the national parks of the country, I attempted to ascertain the average number of parks that Denali tourists had previously visited. Based on sample data, the average calculated was an average of 13.35 national parks previously visited. Additionally, the majority of the visitors had previously visited ten or more national parks. This figure reveals the self-selected nature of the visitors and confirms that their Denali visit can be placed within a larger context. Most people, however, were making their first trip to this particular park, confirming the trend previously identified by the earlier questionnaire.

When canvassed about their motivations for traveling to Denali, visitors provided the following explanations, many of which are closely related. (1) "Denali has the reputation of being the most 'natural' of any park in the U.S. national park system." (2) "It is 'supposedly' the pride of the National Park System." (3) "I sought refuge from the hectic life of the city." (4) "I wanted to see virgin land that is part of the last frontier." (5) "I wanted to see the wildlife." (6) "I heard of the unparalleled scenic beauty." (7) "I wanted to see the majestic mountains." (8) "I just wanted to get away from it all." (9) "I wanted to see and experience pristine wilderness."

All of the above explanations suggest high expectations based on information acquired via word of mouth; seeing pictures and descriptions in travel brochures; reading accounts in literature and popular books; viewing television programs or videos; and to a lesser degree, previous experience. All of the motivations are based on the visual aspects of the park, specifically its scenic beauty and undisturbed wildlife within a context that is without any human imprint and is perceived to have retained its pristine state.

In ascertaining which features of the natural setting visitors found especially attractive, I anticipated a variety of responses, yet the following exhibit more unity than diversity. Several aspects were listed numerous times, including (1) the great physical diversity, especially the mountains, tundra, and braided rivers; (2) wildlife that is abundant, undisturbed, symbolic, and in a natural setting; (3) vastness, immensity, and wide-open space; (4) pristine wilderness; (5) no trails, fences, or any other human imprint; (6) the overpowering visual aspect of the park; (7) clean air and unlimited daylight; (8) the scenic beauty; (9) remoteness; the feel of being "away from it all"; and (10) no noise, traffic, pollution, or commercialization, just peace and tranquillity. These responses indicate an appreciation for a setting that is uninhibiting, aesthetically pleasing, natural, and harmonious.

Denali proved to be more than accommodating when it

came to satisfying the average tourist's quest for uniqueness. Indeed, most visitors claimed that "almost every aspect of the natural setting seemed unique." Additional emphasis was placed on the appeal of (1) vastness, openness, wide-open space; (2) no human imprint or interference (land that appears untouched by humans); (3) undisturbed wildlife (animals that are truly wild, yet not alarmed by visitors); (4) the physical setting (braided rivers, dominant mountains, tundra, glaciers, and extended daylight); (5) the lack of noise, pollution, traffic, and other human impacts; (6) unique management practices and a true wilderness ethic; (7) a truly virgin land that belongs to the wildlife and where people are privileged visitors; (8) continuous unspoiled vistas; and (9) preservation in action (an atmosphere of peace, tranquility, and harmony—a perfect balance between people and nature). These observations serve to distinguish Denali as a place that provides a heightened and fulfilling encounter with nature. More important, they contribute to the specificity of the place.

When asked to compare Denali with other national parks, visitors gave the following typical responses, which again reveal a number of common linkages. (1) Denali stands alone at the top of the hierarchy of national parks; it is the ultimate national park. (2) Unlike other national parks, it is trail-less, uninhibiting, wild, and adventurous. (3) In Denali, we have avoided the mistakes made in our other parks throughout the lower 48. (4) The park appears untouched and totally natural, enabling one to forget that other humans even exist. (5) Denali is more diverse and unpredictable. (6) The park provides more authentic experiences with wildlife. (7) Denali is special because of the respect for the environment and wildlife that people practice here. (8) This park is better managed and controlled. (9) The park is quieter, more peaceful and tranquil. (10) Denali stands alone in terms of its scenic beauty; mainly because there is more of it and you can see more. (11) I think Denali is more in line with the true spirit of conservation. (12) Denali is vast, more expansive, and far more open. (13) The park is totally different because of the lack of people, cars, manmade structures, and commercialization.

These sentiments demonstrate that visitors value the wildness and true wilderness spirit of Denali. Most are not aware, however, that the park benefited from its distant and historically inaccessible location such that development and environmental degradation never preceded sound management practices.

When specifically asked if Denali should be managed differently from other national parks, the visitor consensus was "yes, definitely!" Respondents further elaborated as follows. "Denali is a "one of a kind" national park, and so it requires its own management strategy. Its uniqueness demands our protection and efforts should be made to maintain the park in its pristine state. The system of educating visitors, controlling access, and using the shuttle bus have proven effective and must continue. Manage Denali to ensure it can resist change. As the last intact ecosystem of any substantial size in the U.S., Denali must not be turned into a Yellowstone, Yosemite, or just another great National Park."

"Where possible, other parks should adopt aspects of Denali's management strategy. The perfectly balanced management strategy has made this park different. Others should strive to emulate Denali."

The above contentions claim that Denali should be managed differently because it is in fact different. The management strategy in Denali is perceived to be a resounding success and its tenets should be extended to other national parks.

In an attempt to validate claims made the previous summer, I asked visitors if they felt better after their experience in Denali. Additionally, they were asked to explain in what regard (physically, mentally, spiritually, or some combination) and to venture whether they considered this to be a therapeutic experience. Supporting the results from the previous summer, visitors were unanimous in claiming that they "felt better" in many respects: mentally, physically, and spiritually. The following two explanations elaborate on the experience.

"I felt better mentally, physically, and spiritually. The experience was uplifting. It got me back to a form of nature that I didn't know still existed. This experience provided me with images I will never forget. This is an intense place, a land of extremes, which gives me a heightened awareness. I've never seen so much life in such perfect harmony."

"My experience was therapeutic in many respects. It was refreshing, peaceful, tranquil, and restorative. The peace and tranquillity takes you away from the day to day stress. Long hours of daylight give me a surge of physical energy, yet wilderness vistas provide me with a spiritual peace."

These sentiments suggest an authentically perceived encounter with nature that produces a profound physical, mental, and spiritual impact and has the potential to be a memorable experience. It would be difficult, if not impossible, to substantiate physical, mental, or spiritual healing among visitors. Similarly, it would be a tremendous challenge to try to isolate the specific aspect (physical, mental, or spiritual) of healing that contributes most to one's therapeutic experience. Nevertheless, visitors undoubtedly perceive their Denali experience to be therapeutic. Denali's characterization as a "therapeutic landscape" undeniably contributes to the spirit of the place, and specifically to its reputation as a "place of health."

Based on repetitive concerns regarding the impact of future developments in the park, such as paving the Park Road or building a commercial hotel at Eielson, visitors were asked if such developments would have a positive or negative impact on their experience or image of the park. They were also questioned about whether such developments would affect their decision to visit the park again. The overwhelming majority of the visitors were alarmed by the mere mention of any prospect of development within the park. The following are typical responses.

"Any development beyond maintaining the status quo

would have a profound negative impact on my experience and the image of the park, and would convince me to never return. I don't want to replace the memories I will take from this place."

"Any development will have an adverse and irreversible impact on this special place where a perfect balance now exists, and would deprive future visitors of the ultimate wilderness experience which current visitors now enjoy here."

"Any development would have a negative impact on this truly natural place. It would change the very things that I have come to value most about Denali: the lack of human imprint, the true wilderness, the undisturbed natural setting."

"Any development would serve to destroy Denali's most distinguishing characteristics. Development of any kind would make this unique place just another national park."

"How can anyone even consider changing the only park of its kind? Any development whatsoever would forever change the character of this park."

The more immediate concern of upgrading the Park Road prompted the following realizations. "The underdeveloped nature of the road contributes to the wilderness experience. Visitors perceive the road as primitive, dangerous, adventurous and truly memorable. It blends in well with the wildness of the park, it respects the "lay of the land," and it doesn't appear to be detrimental to the habitat in any way." While visitors welcomed any prospects for improving their view from the bus (i.e., larger windows), they flatly rejected any proposed changes to the nature of the road.

These perspectives express a genuine concern for maintaining the unique character of Denali. Visitors perceive that any alteration to this delicately balanced system will have an adverse affect on the image of this special place and would detract from visitors' experience. Subsequent questionnaires and interviews reaffirmed several of the conclusions that were based on the initial fieldwork. The more recent questionnaire and interviews also add depth in several areas and reveal a visitor commitment to maintain the place in its current state by resisting any proposed changes.

Denali as a Therapeutic Landscape

Perhaps the most intriguing insight that I have gained from questionnaires and from talking to countless visitors is that most people recognize a therapeutic aspect of their Denali experience. Lourdes, France; Bath, England; and Epidauros, Greece, are examples of well-known and historical healing sites. This surely does not exhaust the list of therapeutic landscapes, nor does it imply that such places are site specific. Of a more general nature, mineral springs, spas, mountain retreats, and religious shrines are distributed throughout the globe, and all provide therapeutic experiences to many who use them. It could be a matter of myth, legacy, or elitism that separates the former from the latter. Or it could be that the former invoke a powerful and almost mystical sense of place, and combine with the expectations that are built up along one's journey (or pilgrimage) to ultimately contribute to what is perceived as an authentic experience. Location is thus important, not in the absolute sense, but in the sense that it refers to a specific kind of setting or place that is given preeminence in terms of its therapeutic qualities.

Whereas most conceptions of therapeutic landscapes focus on the built aspects of the cultural landscape, I believe that the notion of therapeutic landscapes as settings for therapeutic experiences can be extended to include totally natural landscapes. In my view, a therapeutic landscape is a place of health that enhances intense relaxation and restoration and facilitates some combination of physical, mental, and spiritual healing. As such, my intent has been to examine the factors that contribute to the healing reputation of Denali National Park.

A review of the literature on Denali provides several insights that collectively emphasize the spirit of the place, the significance of the pristine setting for human-environment interaction, and the park's reputation as a therapeutic landscape. In her book *The Nature of Denali*, Sheri Forbes explains her feelings as she walks along a trail to Horseshoe Lake (an oxbow lake, only about one mile from the park entrance). Forbes recalls: "As you follow the trail to the lake, the human-caused sights and sounds that surround you will be gradually replaced by the signs of nature, and you'll enter a realm where the body can relax, the mind can expand, and the spirit can be restored."[10]

Aldoph Murie provided similar thought-provoking messages of inspiration. Between 1929 and 1970, Murie spent over twenty-five summers conducting research in Denali and is internationally known for his research and writings. Recognized as the foremost researcher of the ecology of Denali National Park, Murie articulated his sentiments about Denali as follows. "Most of us feel with Thoreau that the wilderness is near as well as dear to every man. We come to Denali to watch; to catch a glimpse of the primeval. We come close to the tundra flowers, the lichens, and the animal life. Each of us will take some inspiration home; a touch of tundra will enter our lives and, deep inside, make of us all poets and kindred spirits."[11] Although the term "therapeutic landscape" was not coined when Murie initially wrote the above passage in 1962, his description effectively captures the essence of a therapeutic experience made possible in Denali.

In "Denali: A Peaceable Kingdom," Dale Brown, a writer and explorer for *National Geographic Traveler* recalls, "I came to Denali tired, in need of change. What I found invigorated me, filled me with happiness as warm as sunlight."[12] Douglas Chadwick, an explorer and writer for *National Geographic*, made similar observations during his summer visit. He recalls, "Denali gave me everything one could hope for from a wild place. Then it gave me more than I knew how to hope for: new ways of seeing, feeling and knowing that spring from direct contact with grand natural patterns."[13] In both cases, these

well-traveled writers express the therapeutic effect that Denali
had on them. Thanks to hundreds of questionnaires and dozens
of interviews, I was able to confirm these same sentiments
among a substantial number of visitors during the summers of
1993 and 1994.

Statistics provided by the Park Service at Denali reveal that
more than two-thirds of the visits to the park can be classified
as "non-recreational" visits. With total park visits averaging
1,586,356 per year since 1987, average non-recreational visits
have amounted to 1,033,539 annually.[14] The conclusion
reached by the Park Service is that most people come to Denali
to simply look, relax, and get away from it all. Another
revealing statistic relates to medical care provided to park
visitors. Although the park had 1,397,143 visitors in 1991, and
1,284,730 in 1992, medical care was provided to only 44
people in 1991 (about .00003 percent), and 36 visitors in 1992
(.000028 percent).[15] When one considers that the average age
among park visitors is fifty-seven, these figures take on even
greater significance. Moreover, most of those people injured or
ill were mountain climbers on Mount McKinley, not typical
visitors. Because of the extremely limited demand for medical
care, this "place of health" has no medical facilities. Park
rangers are responsible for the immediate emergency care of
visitors who are ill or injured.

Reflections of the native Athapaskan Indians also enhance
Denali's reputation as a therapeutic landscape. Rick McIntyre
captures some of the folklore and legend surrounding
Denali/Mount McKinley in *Denali Park: An Island in Time*.
According to Athapaskan tales, a group of hunters had camped
to the south of Denali during one of the longest days of the
summer, when they noticed the setting sun disappearing behind
the western flanks of the mountain. A few hours later, they saw
the sun rise out of Denali's eastern slope. Upon returning to
their village, the hunters reported to their chief: "Surely we
have found the home of the sun, as we saw with our own eyes
the sun go into the mountain, and saw it leave its home in the

morning."[16] Since most park visitors come to Denali during the summer months, they too must feel they have found the home of the sun; daylight reigns for all but a couple of hours each day, a sensation that truly appears to "energize" visitors to interior Alaska.

The Koyukon Indians have a perception of the natural environment that extends beyond the empirical into the realm of the spiritual.[17] Behavior toward nature is governed by a variety of supernaturally based rules that ensure the well-being of humans and the environment.[18] This symbiotic relationship is based on mutual respect and is extended to visitors of Denali. Either because they are pre-selected or because they are conditioned by law if not by social norms, visitors tend to treat nature with proper care and respect. Hence, they are perceived to be blessed in return with good luck and good health.

The Koyukons also believe the earth itself is the source of preeminent spiritual power (called *sinhtalla*) and serves as the foundation of medicinal power.[19] Moreover, the animals, plants, landforms, air, weather, and sky are spiritually invested.[20] Thus, Denali forms a sacred place, rich in natural beauty and wildlife and harmonious in natural relationships. In the minds of the Koyukons, respect toward these natural phenomena ensures a reciprocal treatment.

Within the literature of cultural geography, there are numerous concepts and themes that can be applied to Denali as a therapeutic landscape. "Valued environment," developed by Gold and Burgess in 1982, is readily applicable to Denali. The authors contend that their conceptualization refocuses attention upon the close and enriching bond between people and the environments they create, inhabit, manipulate, conserve, visit, or even imagine.[21]

Edward Relph provides another useful insight, recognizing that for much of the time, landscapes serve merely as backgrounds to other more important concerns, but they are occasionally brought forward to our awareness.[22] He further asserts that this awareness may arise because we feel healthy and cheerful and the world seems to reflect our happiness.[23] I submit that a reciprocal arrangement exists between visitors and Denali, where stimulating views encourage a response that promotes even greater interaction with the landscape and a heightened awareness.

John Jakle takes exception with those who feel that landscapes cannot be assessed like works of art. He strongly suggests that people do seek visual encounters with landscape to the exclusion of other pursuits, in an effort to enjoy scenery and attain visual satisfaction.[24] I concur that the search for aesthetically pleasing landscapes is a fundamental motivation for visitors to Denali, and that the pleasure derived is a form of therapy.

Topophilia and Biophilia

Whether or not one accepts the characterization of Denali National Park as a therapeutic landscape, at least in the minds of many visitors, one might still be interested in more "scientific" explanations of how a pristine natural setting can contribute to a therapeutic experience. In 1974, Yi-Fu Tuan coined the term "topophilia" to refer to the affective bond between people and place or setting. He contends that people experience different ranges, varieties, and intensities of topophilic sentiments within different environments.[25] Although Tuan admits that topophilia is not the strongest of human emotions, he notes that "when it is compelling we can be sure that the place or environment has become the carrier of emotionally charged events or perceived as a symbol."[26] In this regard, the concept has indisputable relevance to Denali, especially since, as Tuan later notes, "the term topophilia couples sentiment with place."[27] It is difficult to imagine anyone departing Denali without feelings of affection, warmth, and contentment.

Related to topophilia and just as applicable to Denali is the concept of biophilia. Edward O. Wilson initially coined the term in 1984 to describe what he believes to be the innate affinity that humans have for the natural world. Indeed, Wilson goes so far as to conclude that the human tendency to focus on life and lifelike processes may be a biological need, essential to human development as individuals and as a species.[28] Wilson's pioneering efforts have since attracted attention to the "biophilia hypothesis," which suggests that evolution has endowed humans with a genetically based emotional need to be linked with nature.[29] While establishing the genetic aspect of the biophilia hypothesis is beyond the scope of this book, supporters of the hypothesis do shed light on the attraction of pristine wilderness settings like Denali and their value as therapeutic landscapes.

The Cultural Aspect of Denali

By combining perspectives from both traditional and new cultural geography, this book has examined a broader conception of the cultural aspect of Denali. Into the traditional, it has incorporated the visible, material residual of past and present cultures within the context of the cultural landscape. The subtlety of this imprint reveals not only the undeveloped character of the place but the commitment to preserving it in a pristine state.

From this new perspective comes an appreciation for the meanings that people impart to the place. Examining the cultural activities undertaken and the nature of cultural interactions at specific locales within the park also helped in better understanding the visitor experience. The broadened perspective has led to several important conclusions about the cultural component of the place. First, while any visitor's sense of place may be innately personal, similar experiences can contribute to consensus images of a place. The latter becomes evident when reviewing the questionnaire responses provided by bus riders or the interviews provided by hikers and campers.

As mentioned previously, the consensus image of Denali emerges as a summation of what visitors experienced from the various rest stops along the Park Road.

Second, the spirit of a place has a profound and yet similar impact on various groups as well as individuals. Moreover, people contribute to the spirit of the place as well as being affected by it. Characteristics that contribute to the spirit of Denali include various aspects of the unique physical setting, the perception of pristine wilderness, the presence of undisturbed symbolic wildlife, the presence of a healthy environmental ethic, and the park's distant and remote location.

Third, to fully understand how consensus images of the place evolve, one must examine the underlying processes or structures at work. In the case of Denali, the underlying processes do not give rise to any permanent features on the cultural landscape. On the contrary, the processes preclude any visible imprint, yet they contribute to an enduring aspect of the cultural component of Denali. Specifically, the interpretative programs offered in the park enable visitors to better understand and appreciate the scenic wonders and wildlife of the park while enjoying a harmonious relationship with nature. Park rangers are happy to ascertain that the National Park Service's approach to helping each visitor develop a personal environmental ethic is based on the belief that education will enhance understanding, and understanding accompanied by peer pressure will subsequently result in appropriate respect toward nature.

The educational process begins at the visitor access center (VAC), where all visitors initially arrive. Here, visitors are greeted by park rangers, view interpretative displays, listen to briefings, watch slide shows and videos, and read free copies of the park's newspaper and brochure. All of the above are provided by the Park Service and are designed to enhance the visitor experience in the park.

Visitors are taught the appropriate rules and are made aware of constraints and restraints, and yet at the same time they are conditioned to see the positive side of subscribing to a preservationist or conservationist ethic as appropriate. Additionally, safety is always stressed so that visitors can enjoy the wildness of the pristine natural setting yet avoid injury.

The interpretative support, however, does not end at the VAC, which is only the starting point. Once visitors board the shuttle bus and begin their eight- to eleven-hour excursion into the park, they can rely on the bus driver, who uses a microphone to provide a narrative of the trip. Besides directing the riders' attention to points of interest, the driver can position the bus for opportune photographs, yet avoid any disturbance to the flora and fauna. Bus drivers proudly discuss their responsibilities as stewards and not merely transporters.

During the course of the trip, visitors stop at the Eielson Visitor Center, where the National Park Service employs the methods previously used at the VAC to educate visitors. Moreover, Eielson provides a superb setting for experiencing the nature of Denali. Here, on a bluff overlooking the Thorofare River, visitors experience a fabulous view of the Alaska Range featuring Mount McKinley. The visitors are free to roam about in the peaceful and picturesque setting and experience the fruits of their labor, that is, to see the positive results of adopting a healthy environmental ethic and respecting the place as a valued environment.

During the return trip, the bus riders, now fully recognized "insiders," can provide mutual support for maximizing their wilderness experience. All excursions terminate at the VAC, where visitors can ask questions and clarify aspects of the trip. For those staying overnight at the park hotel or at the campgrounds, regularly scheduled interpretative programs continue to present interesting and educational aspects of the park.

One of the most popular and well-attended programs is the sled dog demonstration, which is conducted twice daily at the park's sled dog kennels. Sled dogs are an undisputed part of the lore of the "North Country," and they have played an important role in the park since its establishment in 1917. The park rangers continue to use the sled dogs to patrol the park during the winter months, a practice that is efficient yet environmentally sensitive. The sled dog kennels were in fact among the earliest structures built in the park. The kennels continue to perform their original function and provide an authentic setting for an informative and enjoyable demonstration with the sled dogs (see photograph 4.12).

The interpretative displays and programs that park rangers provide for the visitors afford superb opportunities to better understand the complex yet fragile wilderness setting. These types of interactions are undoubtedly an integral part of the spirit of the place and represent an aspect of the Denali experience that people take with them when they depart.

Photograph 4.12 A view of the kennel facility

Notes

1. Donald W. Meinig, "Cultural Geography," in *Introductory Geography: Viewpoints and Themes*, Association of American Geographers (Washington, D.C.: AAG, 1967), 97-103.

2. William Norton, *Explorations in the Understanding of Landscape: A Cultural Geography* (New York: Greenwood Press, 1989).

3. R. H. Stoddard, B. W. Blouet, and D. J. Wishert, *Human Geography: People, Places and Cultures* (Englewood Cliffs, N.J.: Prentice Hall, 1986), 87.

4. R. J. Johnston, Derek Gregory, and David M. Smith, *The Dictionary of Human Geography* (Oxford: Blackwell Publishers, 1994), 111.

5. James M. Blaut, "Mind and Matter in Cultural Geography," in *Culture, Form, and Place*, ed., Kent Mathewson (Baton Rouge, La.: Geoscience Publications, 1993).

6. Blaut, "Mind and Matter in Cultural Geography," 349.

7. Carl O. Sauer, *The Morphology of Landscape*, vol. 2, no.2 (Berkeley: University of California Publications in Geography, 1925), 46.

8. Fritz Steele, *The Sense of Place* (Boston: CBI Publishing, 1981), 11.

9. J. N. Entrikin, *The Betweenness of Place: Towards a Geography of Modernity* (Baltimore: Johns Hopkins University Press, 1991), 18.

10. Sheri Forbes, *The Nature of Denali* (Denali National Park: Alaska Natural History Association, 1992), 31.

11. Adolph Murie, *Mammals of Denali* (Anchorage: Alaska Natural History Association), 1.

12. Dale M. Brown, "A Peaceable Kingdom," *National Geographic Traveler* 1: 2 (1984), 103.

13. Douglas H. Chadwick, "Denali: Alaska's Wild Heart," *National Geographic* 182: 2 (1992): 63-87.

14. National Park Service, unpublished statistics, 1993. Note that since 1996, the park service has employed a different approach to calculating visitor statistics. Current numbers are considerably less but do not represent a "real" decline in park visitors.

15. Ken Kehrer, Jr., superintendent, Denali National Park, unpublished Park Service information,1993.

16. Rick McIntyre, *Denali National Park: An Island in Time* (Santa Barbara, Calif.: Sequoia Communications, 1986), 22.

17. Richard K. Nelson, *Make Prayers to the Raven* (Chicago: University of Chicago Press, 1983).

18. Nelson, *Make Prayers to the Raven.*

19. Nelson, *Make Prayers to the Raven.*

20. Nelson, *Make Prayers to the Raven.*

21. John R. Gold and Jacquelin A. Burgess, eds., *Valued Environments* (London: Allen & Unwin, 1982).

22. Edward Relph, "Geographical Experiences and Being-in-the-World: The Phenomonological Origins of Geography," in *Dwelling, Place and Environment: Towards a Phenomenology of Person and World*, ed., D. Seamon and R. Mugerauer (Dordecht, Netherlands: Martinus Nijhoff, 1985), 15-31.

23. Relph, "Geographical Experiences and Being-in-the-World."

24. John A. Jakle, *The Visual Elements of Landscape* (Amherst: University of Massachusetts Press, 1987).

25. Yi-Fu Tuan, "Space and Place: Humanistic Perspective," *Progress in Geography* 6: 211-252.

26. Tuan, "Space and Place," 93.

27. Tuan, "Space and Place," 113.

28. Edward O. Wilson, *Biophilia* (Cambridge, Mass.: Harvard University Press, 1984).

29. Stephen R. Kellert and Edward O. Wilson, *The Biophilia Hypothesis* (Washington, D.C.: Island Press, 1993).

5

Conclusion

During my first summer of fieldwork in the park, visitors emphasized "the lack of human imprint" as Denali's most distinguishing feature. This observation prompted two questions. First, why doesn't the present-day park reveal any hints of previous human occupancy? Second, how can any national park of more than eighty years host more than a million visitors annually and still maintain its pristine wilderness character? These questions suggest that Denali is an anomaly among the U.S. national parks and imply that the park has evolved along a dramatically different path than others. Responses to these questions and implications were best provided by reconstructing a past geography of the Denali region.

The historical geography of Denali National Park unveiled the circumstances and processes that enabled the parklands to survive as an intact ecosystem prior to protection by federal legislation and/or present-day management strategies. The Denali region benefited from its remote location for much of its history and from the lessons learned in managing other national parks within the continental United States. In any case, Denali's historical geography explains much of the park's uniqueness, because the present park is the result of past processes, human and natural. As such, the historical perspective reveals the unique evolution of America's accessible wilderness and illuminates those circumstances and factors that enabled Denali to emerge from the pre-park era free of any human imprint, and to accommodate millions of visitors over the past eighty years without sacrificing its pristine wilderness character. These findings are significant in that they have the potential to contribute to improving management practices in other national parks and wilderness areas.

The historical geography of the park also contributes to the spirit of the place. During the course of their visit, tourists become aware of how Denali evolved through space and time. Many also become cognizant of myths, legacies, folklore, and personalities who were instrumental in the early development of the park. A wide range of information sources are available to the visitors, including publications, media presentations, interpretative displays, and even advertisements. Moreover, park rangers, bus drivers and other visitors may often reinforce what one has learned. Historical information thus becomes an integral part of one's knowledge of and attitude toward the place.

The physical geography of the park is of similar value in understanding Denali's enduring spirit of place. Based on attributes of its absolute location, the park is significantly different from other U.S. national parks in terms of its flora, fauna, and landforms. Moreover, its unique climate and symbolic wildlife, and a host of physical phenomena such as permafrost, braided rivers, glacial surges, and alpenglow, invariably satisfy the tourists' quest for the unique while contributing to Denali's distinctive image. These aspects of physical geography contribute to shared images of the place, essentially forming a common bond among millions of tourists who ride the park shuttle bus, and thus have overlapping "activity spaces." This shared experience and consensus image contributes significantly to Denali's enduring spirit of place.

Edward Relph notes that physical appearance, along with activities and meanings, are the raw materials of the identity of places.[1] I suspect the unparalleled physical setting of Denali facilitates the formation of distinct mental constructs of the park, and shared experiences enhance the longevity of those images. The physical geography of Denali, therefore, encourages human interaction, provides an intense experience with nature, and significantly contributes to the enduring sense of place. In one respect, the physical setting undeniably contributes to Denali's spirit and reputation as a therapeutic landscape, while in another, the physical environment serves as the gauge for measuring human impacts throughout the park's history. From yet another perspective, the physical setting provides the context for an actual or perceived wilderness experience.

The impact of Denali's distinctive natural landscapes on the visitor's eventual mental construct of the place cannot be over-emphasized. To clarify, a landscape refers to the assemblage of human and natural phenomena contained within one's field of view out-of-doors.[2] Indeed, for many who experience the park solely via the shuttle bus, *landscapes become place.* Speaking with tourists as they prepare to leave the park, one will invariably encounter visitors who describe Denali as a collage of varied and unique landscapes based on their recollections of specific scenes viewed at each of the rest stops along the Park Road. Although visitors may generally agree about the scenery at different rest stops and from certain vantage points, each individual personally interacts with the natural environment in a different fashion and within the context of his or her own life-world.

Whereas the historical and physical geography of the park can be approached in a traditional geographic fashion, it was necessary to embrace tenets of the "new" cultural geography in order to strengthen the analytical power of the traditional sub-field. A conceptually broader cultural geography provided a more comprehensive and insightful understanding of the visitor experience within Denali by probing into "layers of meaning" well below the superficial layer (see figure 5.1). The various approaches afforded opportunities to consider a wide range of

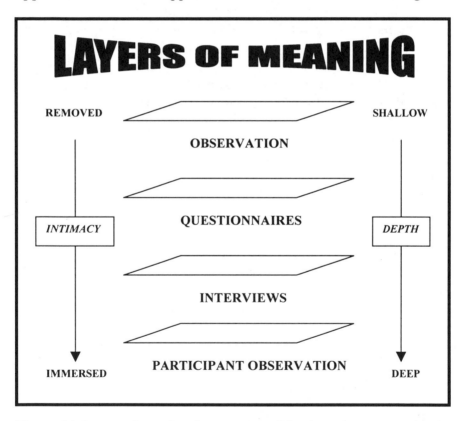

Figure 5.1 Layers of meaning that are accessible via various approaches in humanistic geography

visitor perspectives ranging from the detached outsider's to the immersed insider's point of view. The net result was a greater appreciation of the visitor's sense of place.

This type of humanistic, cultural geography also uncovered the notion of Denali as a therapeutic landscape. It is interesting to note that there has not been a study of Denali, or any other natural setting, as a therapeutic landscape. Consequently, preliminary judgments in this particular area were based on several related sources of information. Special consideration was given to repeated visits and observations by the researcher at the study site. A review of the literature included insights expressed by travelers, researchers, and writers during their visits to Denali. Interviews with park staff members were taken into account. And reflections and attitudes of the native Indians who inhabit the surrounding area were considered. Finally, humanistic perspectives from noted geographers were applied to reinforce or develop key themes.

Thought Provoking Considerations

The visitor experience is rooted in Denali, and the place provides a context for the experience. The experience and place are thus inseparable, a view that has been overlooked in traditional studies of places. Rather than restricting our focus to the *space* of Denali National Park, a specific areal extent of the earth's surface covering more than six million acres, it seems prudent to at least *consider* the conceptual fusion of space and experience that gives to a specific place like Denali a wholeness or individuality.[3] Within the new cultural geography, several concepts appear to offer distinct possibilities for exploring the fusion of space and experience in Denali.

The concepts of cultural hegemony, legitimacy, symbolic landscape, and authenticity have been well established in the

literature of the new cultural geography.[4] These notions are
interrelated and appear to be operative in the park. As a group,
the concepts are worthy of consideration because they poten-
tially enable one to look beyond the empirical aspects of the
place and to better understand the human awareness, agency,
and consciousness in Denali. Specifically, they provide a
mechanism for one to progress beyond traditional empirically
based studies to better comprehend the meaning, value, and
significance of the Denali experience from the visitor's perspective.

Cultural hegemony refers to the capacity of a dominant
group to exercise control, not through overt dominance or
force, but under the guise of a particular cultural, social, or
political practice. In such instances, the group attempts to impose its ideology, values, and beliefs on a subjugated people
who are willing to accept subordinate status. In Denali, one
might consider whether cultural hegemony is implemented via
the visitor indoctrination process, whereby the National Park
Service imposes its conservationist ideology on visitors to the
park through the visitor access system and interpretative programs. Like most hegemonic processes, the indoctrination becomes hidden within the context of the "taken for granted" way
of doing things and providing "services" on a day-to-day basis
in the park.

Legitimacy is closely related to cultural hegemony in that
the National Park Service point of view is presented in terms
of a conservationist ethic. Legitimization occurs because the
goal of developing respect toward nature is perceived by visitors to be a noble one, and because the Park Service uses government publications (brochures, pamphlets, newspapers) and
funding to support its information displays. Legitimization is
enhanced during various phases of the indoctrination process
by relying on specific actors (park rangers, bus drivers, and
guides) to role-play, garner support, and alienate dissenters.

Visitors eventually become role players themselves and use peer pressure to encourage conformity to the group values. Thus, legitimization ensures the persistence of cultural hegemony because the latter is maintained from within the subjugated (visitor) group.

A *symbolic landscape,* or landscape feature, simplifies a complex phenomenon into a specific idea or value.[5] The representative landscape, feature, or object does not have any intrinsic meaning. Rather, people impart meaning and symbolize in an effort to more easily reflect the complicated phenomenon. Denali National Park, as a whole, is a symbolic landscape. It represents the last frontier, nature undisturbed, and pristine, untamed wilderness. The park is replete with creatures symbolic of wildness. The grizzly bear, wolf, golden eagle, and loon are just a few examples. The cultural landscape, however, also reveals symbols that help to impose the cultural hegemony. For instance, the magnificent stained-glass window inside the VAC displays a scene that compels visitors to think about the harmonious relationship between humans and nature that exists within the park. Moreover, the image prompts one to recognize the latter as a safe haven for these endangered species.

Other symbolic aspects of the cultural landscape include the built structures of the park and the Park Road. The buildings of the park are rustic by design, and intended to blend into the natural scenery. The Park Road is symbolic in that it is primitive, adventurous, and respects the lay of the land. The road bridges the gap between civilization and wilderness. Designed with nature's interests in mind, the visitors' long, arduous journey along the primitive road enables them to draw a parallel with the hardships of pilgrims venturing into a sacred land. While the symbols or icons of Denali can appeal to the visitors' emotions and even encourage them to act, the former can also be manipulated by the dominant group. The uniforms of the park rangers engender confidence and professionalism, but also subjugation, and remind us of their role as stewards of nature. Similarly, the ranger cabins remind tourists that the latter are only privileged visitors in the wild land. Thus, the iconography of the Denali landscape is closely tied to the goals of the National Park Service in many regards. Moreover, the symbols are perceived as legitimate and representative of the ideal balance between humans and nature.

Authenticity is the quality of being genuine or bona fide, and pertains to the nature of the Denali experience. In Denali, authenticity is enhanced by the processes of cultural hegemony and legitimization and by the use of symbolism. Visitors (regardless of whether they are classified as hikers, campers, or bus riders) perceive their experience to be a realistic, uninhibited, unparalleled encounter with a wild land. Members of each visitor category acquire legitimacy or validity through mutual reinforcement. Each category of visitor has a common set of goals, and although personal goals may vary slightly among individual members of the group, validation of one's goal attainment must come from other members of the group.

In an effort to impose cultural hegemony over visitors, the Park Service can influence the visitor perspective by manipulating the visitor experience. The latter is most easily accomplished by the use of interpretative programs, which rely heavily on the use of symbols. This celebration of inauthenticity seems justified as a means to simplify and replicate nature and to educate while protecting the fragile environment. The practice provides legitimacy, yet it is invisible to the tourists who *want* to believe that their experience is genuine in all respects. Thus, inauthenticity is a means to achieve cultural hegemony and legitimacy.

The concepts mentioned above are interrelated and arguably present in Denali. They contribute immeasurably to the spirit of the place, yet help one to understand the nature of the

Denali experience. Moreover, they suggest that to fully understand the place, one must consider various layers of meaning beyond the surface layer that can be deduced from empirical observation. While the application of cultural hegemony, legitimacy, symbolic landscape, and authenticity to the Denali experience may stir controversy, the notions are thought-provoking nevertheless and worthy of further examination, at least from an academic perspective.

A Final Thought

The combined effects of Denali's tranquil setting, pristine environment (particularly the air, water, and extended sunlight), undisturbed flora and fauna, and the harmonious social relationships that people develop while riding the shuttle bus appear to enhance Denali's reputation as a therapeutic landscape. The totality of the Denali experience involves both physical and cultural factors combined with historical insights and reputations to provide a setting that is invigorating yet relaxing and restorative. Most visitors anticipate and invariably do have a memorable encounter with nature. They experience and yet contribute to the spirit of Denali while developing an enduring sense of place.

If all places in the world were the same in terms of physical and human phenomena, there would be no geography; but landforms, vegetation, wildlife, and human settlements and activities are not uniformly distributed in space. Thus, the geographer continually seeks to learn what is where and why. In Denali, geography provides a way of looking at and understanding a pristine wilderness setting that, by virtue of its fortuitous history, sub-arctic location, and superb management practices, has no rival among the other U.S. national parks. It is my hope that this geographic perspective enables visitors to couple enjoyment with understanding and to develop a lasting impression of this special place.

Notes

1. Edward Relph, *Place and Placelessness* (London: Pion Ltd., 1976).

2. Eugene J. Palka, "Coming to Grips with the Concept of Landscape," *Landscape Journal* 14, no. 1, 1995, 63-73.

3. J. N. Entrikin. *The Betweenness of Place: Towards a Geography of Modernity* (Baltimore, MD: Johns Hopkins University Press, 1991).

4. Eugene J. Palka, "Accessible Wilderness as a Therapeutic Landscape: The Case of Denali National Park, Alaska," in *Therapeutic Landscapes: The Dynamic Between Place and Wellness*, ed., Allison Williams (Lanham, Md.: University Press of America, 1999). I have previously examined the application of these particular concepts to Denali within the context of this chapter.

5. Dennis Cosgrove, *Social Formation and Symbolic Landscape* (Totowa, N.J.: Barnes & Noble Books, 1985). See also Dennis Cosgrove and Stephen Daniels, eds., *The Iconography of Landscape: Essays on the Symbolic Representation, Design and Use of Past Environments* (Cambridge: Cambridge University Press, 1988).

Bibliography

Agnew, J. A. *Place and Politics: The Geographical Mediation of State and Society*. Boston: Allen and Unwin, 1987.

"An Act To establish the Mount McKinley National Park, in the Territory of Alaska," approved February 26, 1917 (39 Stat. 938).

"An Act To add certain lands to Mount McKinley National Park, Alaska," approved January 30, 1922 (42 Stat. 359).

"An Act To revise the boundary of the Mount McKinley National Park, in the Territory of Alaska, and for other purposes," approved March 19, 1932 (47 Stat. 68).

Alaska Geographic Society. "Major Attraction: Mount McKinley National Park." *Alaska Geographic* 7, no. 1 (1980): 88-95.

_____. "Denali National Park and Preserve." *Alaska Geographic* 8, no. 4 (1981): 36-37.

_____. "Denali Highway." *Alaska Geographic* 10, no. 1 (1983): 123-128.

_____. "Riding the Rails to Denali Country." *Alaska Geographic* 15, no. 3 (1988): 63-68.

_____. "Alaska's Glaciers." *Alaska Geographic* 9, no. 1 (1993).

Alaska Natural History Association. *Denali Alpenglow*. Volume 14 (Summer 1992). Denali National Park, Alaska.

_____. *Denali Alpenglow*. Volume 15 (Summer 1993). Denali National Park, Alaska.

_____. *Denali Alpenglow*. Volume 16 (Summer 1994). Denali National Park, Alaska.

_____. *Denali Alpenglow*, Volume 21, (Summer 1999). Denali National Park, Alaska.

Appleton, Jay. *The Experience of Landscape*. New York: John Wiley and Sons, 1975.

Association of American Geographers. 1968. Field Training in Geography. Technical Paper No. 1. Washington, D.C.: AAG.

Batisse, Michael. "The Biosphere Reserve: A Tool for Environmental Conservation and Management." *Environmental Conservation* 9, no. 2 (1982): 101-111.

_____. "Action Plan for Biosphere Reserves." *Environmental Conservation* 12, no. 1 (1985): 17-27.

Benson, Carl S. "Alaska's Snow." *Weatherwise* 33, no. 5 (1980): 202-206.

Berleant, Arnold. *The Aesthetics of Environment*. Philadelphia: Temple University Press, 1992.

Blaut, James M. "Mind and Matter in Cultural Geography." In *Culture, Form, and Place,* edited by Kent Mathewson. Baton Rouge, La.: Geoscience Publications, 1993.

Bowling, Sue Ann. "The Weather and Climate of Alaska." *Weatherwise* 33, no. 5 (1980): 196-201.

Brease, P. "Geology-Glaciology of the Eielson Vicinity." Unpublished manuscript. Denali National Park, Alaska, 1991.

Brent, Stephen M., and Robert M. Goldberg, eds. *The Alaska Survey and Report: 1970-1971*. Anchorage: Research Institute of Alaska, 1971.

Broek, Jan O. *Geography: Its Scope and Spirit*. Columbus, OH: Charles E. Merrill Books, 1965.

Brooks, A. H. *The Mount McKinley Region, Alaska*. USGS Professional Paper 70. Washington, D.C.: Government Printing Office, 1911.

Brown, Dale M. "A Peaceable Kingdom." *National Geographic Traveler* 1, no. 2 (1984): 103-115.

Brown, William E. *Denali: Symbol of the Alaskan Wild*. Virginia Beach: Donning Company, 1993.

Buskirk, Steve. *Denali: The Story behind the Scenery*. Las Vegas: KC Publications, 1989.

Cameron, Jenks. *The National Park Service: Its History, Activities and Organization*. New York: Prentice Hall, 1922.

Capps, Stephen R. *The Kantishna Region, Alaska*. USGS Bulletin 687. Washington, D.C.: Government Printing Office, 1919.

_____. "The Eastern Portion of Mount McKinley National Park." In *Mineral Resources of Alaska*, Bulletin 836, USDI, USGS. Washington, D.C.: Government Printing Office (1933): 219-300.

_____. *Geology of the Alaska Railroad Region*. USGS Bulletin 907. Washington, D.C.: Government Printing Office, 1940.

Chadwick, Douglas H. "Denali: Alaska's Wild Heart." *National Geographic* 182, no. 2 (1992): 63-87.

Clark, Kenneth M. *Landscape into Art*. London: John Murray, 1949.

Collier, Michael. *The Geology of Denali National Park*. Anchorage, AK: Alaska Natural History Association, 1989.

Coney, P., D. L. Jones, and J. W. H. Monger. "Cordilleran Suspect Terranes." *Nature* 288 (1980): 329-333.

Conzen, Michael P., ed. *The Making of the American Landscape*. London: Harper Collins Academic, 1990.

Coones, Paul. "Landscape Geography." In *The Student's Companion to Geography*, edited by Alisdair Rogers, Heather Viles, and Andrew Goudie. Oxford: Blackwell Publishers, 1992.

_____. "Landscape Studies in Practice." In *The Student's Companion to Geography*, edited by Alisdair Rogers, Heather Viles and Andrew Goudie. Oxford: Blackwell Publishers, 1992.

Cosgrove, Dennis. "Towards a Radical Cultural Geography: Problems of Theory." *Antipode* 15, no. 1 (1983): 1-11.

_____. *Social Formation and Symbolic Landscape.* Totowa, N.J.: Barnes & Noble Books, 1985.

_____. "New Directions in Cultural Geography." *Area* 19, no. 2 (1987): 95-101.

Cosgrove, Dennis, and Stephen Daniels, eds. *The Iconography of Landscape: Essays on the Symbolic Representation, Design and Use of Past Environments.* Cambridge: Cambridge University Press, 1988.

Darby, H. C., ed. *An Historical Geography of England before AD 1800.* Cambridge: Cambridge University Press, 1936.

Davidow, Beth. "The High One." *Earth* 2, no. 5 (1993): 46-51.

Davis, W. M. "The Principles of Geographical Description." *Annals of the Association of American Geographers* 5 (1915): 61-105.

Dilsaver, Lary M., and Craig E. Colten, eds. *The American Environment: Interpretations of Past Geographies.* Lanham, Md.: Rowman & Littlefield, 1992.

Driver, B. L., and S. Ross Tocher. "Toward a Behavioral Interpretation of Recreation Engagements with Implications for Planning." In *Elements of Outdoor Recreation Planning,* edited by B.L. Driver. Ann Arbor: University of Michigan Press, 1975.

Entrikin, J. N. *The Betweenness of Place: Towards a Geography of Modernity.* Baltimore: Johns Hopkins University Press, 1991.

Fischer, Otto. "Landscape as Symbol." *Landscape* 4, no. 3 (1955): 24-33.

Flynn, Jenny. "Denali at 75: From Sheep to Shuttle Buses." *Denali Alpenglow* 14 (Summer 1992): 1.

Forbes, Sheri. *The Nature of Denali.* Denali National Park: Alaska Natural History Association, 1992.

Ford, Jesse, and Barbara L. Bedford. "The Hydrology of Alaskan Wetlands, USA: A Review." *Arctic and Alpine Research* 19, no. 3 (1987): 209-229.

Freeburg, Janie, and Diana Ackland, eds. *Insight Guides: Alaska*. Singapore: APA Publications, 1991.

Friedlander, M. *Landscape, Portrait, Still-Life*. New York: Schocken Books, 1963.

Gallagher, Winifred. *The Power of Place*. New York: Poseidon Press, 1993.

Gesler, Wilbert M. *The Cultural Geography of Health Care*. Pittsburgh: University of Pittsburgh Press, 1991.

_____. "Therapeutic Landscapes: Medical Issues in Light of the New Cultural Geography." *Social Science & Medicine* 34, no.7 (1992): 735-746.

_____. "Therapeutic Landscapes: Theory and a Case Study of Epidauros, Greece." Environment and Planning D: *Society and Space* 11 (1992): 171-189.

Gilbert, Wyatt G. *A Geologic Guide to Mount McKinley National Park*. Anchorage: Alaska Natural History Association, 1979.

Gold, John R., and Jacquelin A. Burgess, eds. *Valued Environments*. London: Allen & Unwin, 1982.

Graef, Kris Valencia (Managing Editor). *The Milepost*. Bothell, Wash.: Alaska Northwest Books, 1992.

Grant, Madison. "The Establishment of Mount McKinley National Park." In *Hunting and Conservation: The Book of the Boone and Crockett Club*, edited by G. B. Grinnell and Charles Sheldon. New Haven: Yale University Press, 1925.

Gregg, William P., Jr., Stanley L. Krugman, and James D. Wood, Jr., eds. *Proceedings of the Symposium on Biosphere Reserves, Fourth World Wilderness Congress*, September 14-17, 1987, YMCA at the Rockies, Estes Park, Colorado, USA. U.S. Department of the Interior, National Park Service, Atlanta, Georgia, 1989, 291 pages.

Greenbie, Barrie B. *Spaces: Dimensions of the Human Landscape*. New Haven: Yale University Press, 1981.

Gregory, Derek. *Ideology, Science and Human Geography*. London: Hutchinson & Co., 1978.

Grigal, D. F. 1979. "Extractable Soil Nutrients and Permafrost under Adjacent Forest Types in Interior Alaska." *Northwest Science* 53, no. 1 (1979): 43-50.

Hamerton, Philip Gilbert. *Landscape*. Boston: Roberts Brothers, 1885.

Hammitt, William E., and David N. Cole. *Wildland Recreation: Ecology and Management*. New York: John Wiley and Sons, 1987.

Harris, Dawn U. *The Geologic Study of the National Parks and More*, 2nd ed. Fort Collins: Colorado State University Press, 1978.

Hartshorne, Richard. *The Nature of Geography*. Lancaster, Pa.: Association of American Geographers, 1939.

Haugen, R. K. *Climate of Remote Areas in North-Central Alaska: 1975-1979 Summary*. Hanover, N.H.: CREEL Report 82-35, 1982.

Heacox, Kim. *The Denali Road Guide*. Denali National Park: Alaska Natural History Association, 1986.

_____. *In Denali*. Santa Barbara, CA: Jane Freeburg, 1992.

Herron, Joseph S. 1899. *Exploration in Alaska*. Washington, D.C.: War Department, 1901.

Hunter, John Michael. *Land into Landscape*. New York: Longman Group, 1985.

Jackson, Edgar L. "Public Views about Resource Development and Preservation: Results from an Alberta Study." *The Canadian Geographer* 33, no. 2 (1989): 163-168.

Jakle, John A. *The Visual Elements of Landscape*. Amherst: University of Massachusetts Press, 1987.

James, Preston E. "The Terminology of Regional Description." *Annals of the Association of American Geographers* 24, no. 2 (1934): 78-92.

Johnston, R. J. *A Question of Place*. Oxford: Blackwell Publishers, 1991.

_____. *Geography and Geographers*, 4th ed. London: Edward Arnold, 1991.

Johnston, R. J., Derek Gregory, and David M. Smith. *The Dictionary of Human Geography*, 3rd ed. Oxford: Blackwell

Publishers, 1994.

Jones, Kelvyn and Graham Moon. "Medical Geography: Taking Space Seriously." *Progress in Human Geography* 17, no. 4 (1993): 515-524.

Kearns, Robin A. "The Place of Health in the Health of Place: The Case of the Hokianga Special Medical Area." *Social Science & Medicine* 33, no. 4 (1991): 519-530.

_____. "Place and Health: Toward a Reformed Medical Geography." *The Professional Geographer* 45, no. 2 (1993): 139-147.

Kehrer, Ken, Jr., Superintendent, Denali National Park. Unpublished Park Service information on medical treatment in Denali in 1991 and 1992.

Kellert, Stephen R., and Edward O. Wilson. *The Biophilia Hypothesis*. Washington, D.C.: Island Press, 1993.

Kertell, Kenneth, and Alan Seegert. *Denali National Park Bird Finding Guide*. Denali National Park: Alaska Natural History Association, 1984.

Lanphere, M. A., and B. L. Reed. "The McKinley Sequence of Granitic Rocks: A Key Element in the Accretionary History of Southern Alaska." *Journal of Geophysical Research* 90 (1985): 413-21, 430.

Loeb, Charlie. "Wildlife from the Bus Window." *Denali Alpenglow* Vol. 14 (Summer 1992): 7.

Lunde, Eleanor. Personal interviews. Chapel Hill, N.C., 1994.

MacEwen, A., and M. MacEwen. *National Parks: Conservation or Cosmetics?* London: Allen & Unwin, 1982.

Machlis, Gary E., and Danna E. Dolsen. *Visitor Services Project Report 18: Denali National Park and Preserve*. University of Idaho, College of Forestry, February 1989.

Makowski, Ellen Huening. *Scenic Parks and Landscape Values*. New York: Garland Publishing, 1990.

Marsh, William M., and Jeff Dozier. *Landscape: An Introduction to Physical Geography*. Reading, Mass.: Addison-Wesley, 1981.

Mattern, Hermann. "The Growth of Landscape Consciousness." *Landscape* 15, no. 3 (1966): 14-20.

Mayhew, Susan and Penny Anne. *The Concise Oxford Dictionary of Geography*. Oxford: Oxford University Press, 1992.

McHarg, Ian L. *Design with Nature*. Garden City, N.Y.: The Natural History Press, 1969.

McIntyre, Rick. *Denali National Park: An Island in Time*. Santa Barbara, CA: Sequoia Communications, 1986.

Meinig, Donald W. "Cultural Geography." In *Introductory Geography: Viewpoints and Themes*. Washington, D.C.: Association of American Geographers, 1967.

Meinig, D.W., ed. *The Interpretation of Ordinary Landscapes*. Oxford: Oxford University Press, Inc., 1979a.

Mikesell, Marvin. "Landscape." In *International Encyclopedia of the Social Sciences*, Volume 8. 575-580. New York: Crowell-Collier and Macmillan, 1968.

Morgan, Lael. "Alaska's Native People." *Alaska Geographic* 6, no. 3 (1979).

Murie, Adolph. *The Grizzlies of Mount McKinley*. USDI, NPS, Scientific Monograph Series no. 14. Washington, DC: Government Printing Office, 1981.

———. *Mammals of Denali*. 5th ed. Anchorage: Alaska Natural History Association, 1983.

Nash, R. "The American Invention of National Parks." *American Quarterly* 22 (1970): 726-735.

National Park Service. Unpublished statistics of visitors to Denali National Park and Preserve, 1940-1992. Denali National Park, Alaska, 1993.

Nelson, F., and S. I. Outcalt. "Anthropogenic Geomorphology in Northern Alaska." *Physical Geography* 3, no. 1 (1982): 17-48.

Nelson, Richard K. *Make Prayers to the Raven*. Chicago: University of Chicago Press, 1983.

Nierenberg, Jon. *A Backcountry Companion for Denali National Park*. Anchorage: Alaska Natural History Association, 1994.

Norton, William. "Humans, Land, and Landscape: A Proposal for Cultural Geography." *The Canadian Geographer* 31, no. 1 (1987): 21-30.

_____. *Explorations in the Understanding of Landscape: A Cultural Geography*. New York: Greenwood Press, 1989.

Ostrem, G., N. Haakensen, and T. Eriksson. "The Glaciation Level in Southern Alaska." *Geografiska Annaler* 63A, nos. 3-4 (1981): 251-260.

Palka, Eugene J. "America's Accessible Wilderness: An Historical Geography of Denali National Park." *Historical Geography* 24, nos. 1 & 2 (1995): 107-125.

_____. "Coming to Grips with the Concept of Landscape." *Landscape Journal* 14, no. 1 (1995): 63-73.

_____. "Accessible Wilderness as a Therapeutic Landscape: The Case of Denali National Park, Alaska." In *Therapeutic Landscapes: The Dynamic Between Place and Wellness*, edited by Allison Williams. Lanham, Md.: University Press of America, 1999.

Pocock, D. C. D., ed. *Humanistic Approaches in Geography*. Durham: Department of Geography, University of Durham, 1988.

_____. "Literature and Humanist Geography." *Area* 17, no. 2 (1985): 117-122.

_____. *Landscapes of the Mind*. Toronto: University of Toronto Press, 1990.

Post, Austin S. "The Exceptional Advances of the Muldrow, Black Rapids and Susitna Glaciers." *Journal of Geophysical Research* 65, no. 11 (1960): 3703-3712.

Pratt, Verna E., and Frank G. Pratt. *Wildflowers of Denali National Park*. Anchorage: Alaskakrafts, Inc., 1993.

Pred, A. R. "Place as Historically Contingent Process." *Annals of the Association of American Geographers* 74 (1984): 279-97.

President of the United States of America. A Proclamation. Denali National Monument. Proclamation 4616, December 1, 1978.

Price, Marie, and Martin Lewis. "The Reinvention of Cultural Geography." *Annals of the Association of American Geographers* 83 (1993): 1-17.

Relph, Edward. *Place and Placelessness*. London: Pion, 1976.

_____. *Rational Landscapes and Humanistic Geography*. London: Croom Helm, 1981.

_____. "Geographical Experiences and Being-in-the-World: The Phenomenological Origins of Geography." In *Dwelling, Place and Environment: Towards a Phenomenology of Person and World*, edited by D. Seamon and R. Mugerauer. Dordrecht, Netherlands: Martinus Nijhoff, 1985.

Rhode, Elaine. "Denali Country." *Alaska Geographic* 15, no. 3 (1988): 6-21.

Rowntree, L.C. and Conkey, M.W. "Symbolism and the Cultural Landscape." *Annals of the Association of American Geographers* 70 (1980): 459-474.

Rowntree, Lester B., Kenneth E. Foote, and Mona Domosh. "Cultural Geography." In *Geography in America*, edited by Gary L. Gaile and Cort J. Willmott. Columbus, Ohio: Merrill Publishing, 1989.

Runte, A. *The National Parks: The American Experience*. Lincoln: University of Nebraska Press, 1979.

Sadler, Barry, and Allen Carlson, eds. *Environmental Aesthetics: Essays in Interpretation*. Victoria, B.C.: University of Victoria, Department of Geography, 1982.

Sauer, Carl O. *The Morphology of Landscape*. Berkeley: University of California Publications in Geography, vol. 2, no. 2, 1925.

_____. "The Morphology of Landscape." Reprinted in *Land and Life: A Selection from the Writings of Carl Ortwin Sauer*, edited by John Leighly. Berkeley: University of California Press, 1963.

Schlereth, Thomas J., ed. *Material Culture: A Research Guide*. Lawrence: University Press of Kansas, 1985.

Schmitt, Judi. SAR LOG. *Response* 11, no. 4 (1992): 30-32.

Seamon, David. "Community, Place and Environment." In *The*

Human Experience of Space and Place, edited by Anne Buttimer and David Seamon. New York: St. Martin's Press, 1980.

Sheldon, Charles. *The Wilderness of Denali*. New York: Scribner's, 1930.

Small, John, and Michael Witherick. *A Modern Dictionary of Geography*. London: Edward Arnold Publishers, 1986.

Squire, Shelagh J. "Accounting for Cultural Meanings: The Interface between Geography and Tourism Studies Reexamined." *Progress in Human Geography* 18, no. 1 (1994): 1-16.

Steele, Fritz. *The Sense of Place*. Boston: CBI Publishing, 1981.

Stilgoe, John R. *Common Landscape of America, 1580 to 1845*. New Haven: Yale University Press, 1982.

Stoddard, R. H., B. W. Blouet, and D. J. Wishart. *Human Geography: People, Places and Culture*. Englewood Cliffs, N.J.: Prentice Hall, 1986.

Stone, D. B. and W. K. Wallace. "A Geological Framework of Alaska." *Episodes* 10, no. 4 (1987): 283-289.

Stout, James H., and Clement G. Chase. "Plate Kinematics of the Denali Fault System." *Canadian Journal of Earth Sciences* 17, no. 11 (1980): 1527-1537.

Strong, Douglas Hillman. "The Rise of American Aesthetic Conservation: Muir, Mather, and Udall." *National Parks Magazine* 44, no. 269 (1970): 5-9.

Tuan, Yi-Fu. "Space and Place: Humanistic Perspective." *Progress in Geography* 6 (1974): 211-252.

_____. *Topophilia: A Study of Environmental Attitudes, Perceptions and Values*. Englewood Cliffs, N.J.: Prentice Hall, 1974.

U.S. Department of the Interior. *The Alaska Railroad Travelogue*. "Mt. McKinley Park Route." Washington, D.C.: Government Printing Office, 1928.

_____. *Annual Report(s) of the Governor of Alaska to the Secretary of the Interior, 1941-1949*. Washington, D.C.:

Government Printing Office, 1941-49.

_____. *Annual Report(s) of the Governor of Alaska to the Secretary of the Interior, 1950-1958.* Washington, D.C.: Government Printing Office, 1950-58.

_____. *Report of the Director of the National Park Service to the Secretary of the Interior for the Fiscal Year Ended June 30, 1921 and the Travel Season 1921.* Washington, D.C.: Government Printing Office, 1921.

_____. *Report of the Director of the National Park Service to the Secretary of the Interior for the Fiscal Year Ended June 30, 1922 and the Travel Season 1922.* Washington, D.C.: Government Printing Office, 1922.

_____. *Report of the Director of the National Park Service to the Secretary of the Interior for the Fiscal Year Ended June 30, 1923 and the Travel Season 1923.* Washington, D.C.: Government Printing Office, 1923.

_____. *Report(s) of the Governor of Alaska of the Secretary of the Interior, 1921-1925.* Washington, D.C.: Government Printing Office, 1921-25.

U.S. Department of the Interior, National Park Service. *Denali National Park and Preserve.* Brochure and Map. Washington, D.C.: Government Printing Office, 1992.

_____. *Denali National Park and Preserve, Alaska, General Management Plan, Land Protection Plan, and Wilderness Suitability Review.* Washington, D.C.: Government Printing Office, 1987.

_____. *Land Use in the North Additions of Denali National Park and Preserve: An Historical Perspective.* Research/Resources Management Report AR-9. Anchorage, AK: NPS, Anchorage Regional Office, 1989.

_____. *Laws Relating to the National Parks and Monuments.* Washington, D.C.: Government Printing Office, 1933.

_____. *Proceedings of the National Park Conference, January 2-6, 1917.* Washington, D.C.: Government Printing Office, 1917.

U.S. House, 64th Congress, 1st Session. May 4, 1916. "Hear-

ing on a Bill to Establish Mount McKinley National Park."
Washington, D.C.: Government Printing Office.

U.S. House, 64th Congress, 2nd Session. January 10, 1917.
H.R. 1273. "Mount McKinley National Park, Alaska."
Washington, D.C.: Government Printing Office.

U.S. House, 96th Congress, 1st Session. February 1, 6, 7, 8,
and 13, 1979. "Alaska National Interest Lands Conservation Act of 1979," Hearings before the committee on Interior and Insular Affairs, House of Representatives, on H.R.
39. Washington, D.C.: Government Printing Office.

U.S. House, 97th Congress, 1st Session. 1981. H.R. 97-207.
"Providing for the retention of the name of Mount McKin-
ley: report to accompany H.R. 772." Washington, D.C.:
Government Printing Office.

U.S. Senate, 56th Congress, 1st Session. 1900. S.R. 1023.
"Compilation of Narratives of Exploration of Alaska."
Washington, D.C.: Government Printing Office.

U.S. Senate, 64th Congress, 1st Session. 1916. S.R. 622. "National Park Service."   Washington, D.C.: Government
Printing Office.

U.S. Senate, 64th Congress, 1st Session. May 5, 1916. "Hearing on the Establishment of Mount McKinley National
Park." Washington, D.C.: Government Printing Office.

Wahrhaftig, Clyde. "The Alaska Range." In *Landscapes of
Alaska: Their Geologic Evolution*, edited by Howel Williams. Berkeley: University of California Press, 1958.

Wilson, Edward O. *Biophilia*. Cambridge, Mass.: Harvard
University Press, 1984.

Winchell, Dick G. "Design Context, Design Concepts: Critical
Components of Park Planning." *Journal of Park and Recreation Administration* 9, no. 1 (1991): 65-74.

Wuerthner, George. *Alaska's Mountain Ranges*. Helena, Mt.:
American Geographic Publishing, 1988.

Index

About the Author

Eugene J. Palka is associate professor and the director of the Geography Program at the United States Military Academy at West Point. He has a master's degree in geography from Ohio University and a doctorate from the University of North Carolina at Chapel Hill. He has previously authored a book, two instructor's manuals to accompany college textbooks, a four-volume bibliography of military geography, several book chapters, and more than twenty-five articles on various aspects of cultural, historical, and military geography. His infatuation with Denali National Park began during an army tour in Alaska and was pursued in earnest during his doctorate program at UNC.

Modern Critical Views

T.S. ELIOT

Edited with an introduction by

Harold Bloom

Sterling Professor of the Humanities
Yale University

1985
CHELSEA HOUSE PUBLISHERS
New York

PROJECT EDITORS: Emily Bestler, James Uebbing
EDITORIAL COORDINATOR: Karyn Browne
EDITORIAL STAFF: Joy Johannessen, Sally Stepanek, Linda Grossman
RESEARCH: Kevin Pask
DESIGN: Susan Lusk

Cover illustration by Kye Carbone
Composition provided by Collage Publications, Inc., New York

Printed and bound in the United States of America

Library of Congress Cataloging in Publication Data
T.S. Eliot, modern critical views.
    Bibliography: p.
    Contents: Introduction/Harold Bloom—
Ash-Wednesday/Hugh Kenner—Antique drum/Northrup Frye—[etc.]
    1. Eliot, T.S. (Thomas Stearns), 1888–1965—Criticism
and interpretation—Addresses, essays, lectures.
I. Bloom, Harold.
PS3509.L43Z8726   1984   821'.912   84-22930
ISBN 0–87754–601–0

Chelsea House Publishers
Harold Steinberg, Chairman & Publisher
Susan Lusk, Vice President
A Division of Chelsea House Educational Communications, Inc.
133 Christopher Street, New York, NY 10014

Contents